GAME CHANGER

HOW TO BE 10x IN THE TALENT ECONOMY

GAME
CHANGER

MICHAEL
SOLOMON

RISHON
BLUMBERG

with DANIEL WEIZMANN

HARPERCOLLINS
LEADERSHIP

AN IMPRINT OF HARPERCOLLINS

Published by HarperCollins Leadership, an imprint of HarperCollins Focus LLC.

Book design by Aubrey Khan, Neuwirth & Associates.

Any internet addresses, phone numbers, or company or product information printed in this book are offered as a resource and are not intended in any way to be or to imply an endorsement by HarperCollins Leadership, nor does HarperCollins Leadership vouch for the existence, content, or services of these sites, phone numbers, companies, or products beyond the life of this book.

ISBN 978-1-4002-1860-8 (eBook)
ISBN 978-1-4002-1870-7 (HC)

Library of Congress Control Number: 2020938380

Printed in the United States of America
20 21 22 23 LSC 10 9 8 7 6 5 4 3 2 1

This book is dedicated to our wives, Jenny Solomon and Isabel Blumberg, and our children, Alec Blumberg, Lucy Solomon, Luke Blumberg, and Rainen Solomon.

CONTENTS

PART ONE
HOW TO BECOME A 10x COMPANY AND ATTRACT 10x TALENT

PART TWO
HOW YOU CAN BECOME 10x

CONTENTS

FOREWORD

When we first conceived of this book in late 2018, it was because we knew that rapid advances in technology had radically transformed working life in a way that not everybody was acclimating to at the same rate. As managers of top tech talent, we wanted to create a book that would help educate readers of all stripes.

Little did we know as we finished this manuscript and handed it in to our publisher for final edits in preparation for a fall 2020 release that the world that we thought had changed drastically was about to show us what real drastic change is.

The stories in this book and the lessons we convey are no less important now than they were a year ago, but one major element has changed. Though we talk about it a fair amount in the book, this one change necessitates that we write this "Foreword" now—remote work.

Among the big items we knew we had to share was the usefulness and, in fact, the necessity of remote work. We believed and still believe that the ability to solve big problems remotely is one of the twenty-first century's greatest gifts.

Little did we know that the onslaught of COVID-19 would soon expose how unprepared the world is for remote work on a grand scale. The ability of companies and governments, small and large, to swiftly and efficiently deploy remote working capabilities on a global scale is now essential. Moreover, remote work is no longer just a preference for top 10x tech talent. As we have learned, it can be a matter of life and death, success and failure, for everyone.

So, as you read this book, keep the concept of remote work close to the forefront of your mind. It, and the other lessons in this book, are the new normal.

As we write this "Foreword," Rishon is in Miami with his two sons, while his wife is working on the frontlines in New York City taking care of patients—seeing some for the first time now via telemedicine. In both cities, all restaurants are closed except for take-out. In Miami, beaches, and all the other things that make Miami a thriving and wonderful outdoor metropolis, are shut down.

Nonetheless, the two of us in Miami and Montclair, New Jersey, our wonderful 10x team from upstate New York, Brooklyn, Queens, and Manhattan, and the amazing 10x talent we represent hailing from all places near and far are all still hard at work. Sure, we've had to add a few more cloud-based tools to our arsenal to make things run more smoothly, but business carries on. Thankfully, we were well prepared to work remotely, and we are all adjusting to this period of social distancing.

This is our new world. And it is quite different from the world we lived in just a few weeks ago. Things will return to normal, or at least a new normal, and when they do, we will all be better prepared.

In the meantime, we hope you, your families, and your teams are safe and healthy.

Rishon Blumberg and Michael Solomon
March 2020

INTRO~~OUTRO~~

WHAT WE MEAN
WHEN WE SAY "10x"

WE LIVE IN A 10x WORLD

Welcome to the era of 10x talent, where businesses and governments, large and small, are only as good as their very best players.

Today, the exceptionally talented matter more than ever—and they know it.

They have changed the game for all time.

With the rapid digitization of every conceivable product and service— in fact, virtually every human action and interaction—the environment has transformed so fast that nearly everyone you deal with has to be phenomenally gifted and ready and willing to work for you.

Turning back is not an option. The 10xers are at the wheel.

So, what do we mean, exactly, when we call someone a 10x talent?

First and foremost, in our experience, we're referring to the world's most sought-after programmers and coding artists, but the 10x concepts we cover in this book will resonate with anyone who cares about exponential self-improvement for themselves or their organization. To be 10x is to be more than great, to deliver more than ten times the expectations. A 10xer is equal parts high IQ and high EQ (emotional quotient; empathy, the ability to recognize and respond to the emotions of oneself and others). A 10xer is in a constant state of evolution and improvement, fueled by curiosity, ambition, and an insatiable desire to do more and do it better. A 10xer is there to tackle your thorniest problems, improve your strongest assets, and cut a path to success.

It's important to note that 10xers come in all shapes, sizes, genders, races, nationalities, sexual orientations, and ages. (We opted to use binary gender pronouns throughout this book for simplicity, but anyone, no matter how they define themselves, can be 10x.)

Whatever your venture, you're going to need as many 10xers as you can get.

> The future is already here—it's just not evenly distributed.
> —WILLIAM GIBSON, 2003

Over the coming decades, as machines replicate more and more physical and intellectual processes, the need for live humans to deliver exponentially beyond expectation is going to increase. It won't be good enough to be good. Good will be easily replaced by algorithms and robots. You're going to need to align with the truly outstanding and, for most of us, that will require a reinvention of mindset. If you're not striving to become a game changer or your company isn't upping its game, the automated future will pass you by.

That's where this book comes in.

From where we stand, the 10x revolution is already well underway.

To even the most casual observer, it's easy to see that traditional work roles are going, going, gone. Old, entrenched hierarchies, hiring practices, production modes, and managerial styles all face imminent extinction. True,

10xers in the tech sphere have been the first to create and embrace this radical paradigm shift, but the big changes are moving like a wildfire through every sector. The old model employee accepted the role of a cog in the machine. Today, 10x talent knows the machine can't work without them, and this one switch fundamentally differentiates the old workplace from the new. Now 10x talent knows that it's on you to get with *their* program.

Tech and digitization have disrupted the very foundation of all ventures, business, government, or otherwise and in so doing have handed over the controls to those who have the exceptional skills to provide efficiency and meaningful growth. The top six companies as measured by market cap are tech companies, and all of the four US companies that have reached trillion-dollar market caps are tech companies. Nine of the twenty richest people in the world today made their money in technology. And the rest of us, for better or worse, work in tech right alongside them. Whether you are a W2 (full-time or part-time employee) or a 1099 (freelance contractor), whatever your industry, whatever your field, you are now living under the early effects of this game-changing 10x revolution.

THE 10x DIFFERENCE

Excellence is being able to perform at a high level over and over again. You can hit a half-court shot once. That's just the luck of the draw. If you consistently do it, that's excellence.
—JAY-Z, 2011

Game Changer is about the dual impact that technology and the people who create it are having on the way companies and governments must approach their greatest asset, their talent. Together, we will uncover the secrets behind 10x performance in any industry, because the ability to attract, hire, and retain 10x talent is a game changer for any company, large or small.

In fact, 10x performance is what you require just to stay in the game.

How literally do we mean that? Here's a real story from the front lines, more typical than you'd imagine.

We were approached last year by a successful, tech-based, nonprofit founder. Let's call her Nicole. She had a technical background, but had long since moved out of that role. Nicole knew we managed the kind of top-level coders who could rebuild her company's product. Since 2011, we've built a reputation for finding, vetting, and matching the finest contract tech talent with companies large and small, everyone from Verizon, eBay, BMW, and Amex to MIT, Vice, and even the federal government.

Nicole confided in us: She knew her thirty-six-member team was simply not delivering the way she needed. We told her we had just the right 10xer for the job and showed her the one person we thought was best suited to lead the project, as well as a couple more developers who could provide the speed and capacity required to turn the company around with finesse.

Nicole liked what she saw—she told us to sit tight for a couple weeks and to not mention our conversation to anyone.

Two weeks later, Nicole returned to our office with the news that she had let go of no less than thirty-three of her thirty-six-person team. *More than 90 percent.* She was sorry to lay off that many fine workers and was quick to mention that they were well taken care of, but there was no way around this one simple fact: Our three recommended 10xers could deliver a better, stronger, more sustainable product than thirty-three or even a hundred engineers who were just "very good."

This is only one story among hundreds, but it neatly demonstrates the true power of 10x in a concrete fashion. Within six months, Nicole's platform was rebuilt with modern everything, as fast at processing transactions as Amazon.com and loaded with new and long-desired features, and Nicole had a new, robust wave of growth on her hands.

Lesson One: In the new talent economy, everybody you deal with better be 10x, or at least striving to be.

EMBRACE 10x OR GET LEFT BEHIND

The game has already changed, but not everyone has acclimated with the same speed or grace. As obvious as the basic fact of the 10x revolution is for us, it has been harder for some to internalize, especially those people working with older, larger entities mired in outmoded policies, bureaucracy, and stagnating cultural standards.

Another true story—the names have been changed but nobody's innocent.

Picture two companies—make that two *desperate* companies: an education start-up and a mid-sized pharmaceutical outfit. They both urgently needed a truly gifted coder to step in and rethink the complex technical elements of their businesses from the ground up, so they reached out to us. After some consideration, we brought forward Jake, one of our very best clients.

Jake was a seasoned developer who exemplified the concept of 10x, delivering value way beyond promises on a regular basis. He knew what he wanted, and it wasn't a full-time W2 job. Jake wanted to work remotely 70 percent of the time. He wanted to give input on the big decisions regarding every build, and he wanted the kind of hourly rate he had become accustomed to as a company-saving, top-shelf programmer. Most of all, Jake knew he was in demand. Every week, we received inquiries for him.

The pharma company, with offices worldwide, balked at Jake's requests. Why couldn't he just be grateful for a real job offer from a solid firm? Why wasn't he overjoyed to take his assigned role in the chain of command? The hiring powers could not understand what Jake was after and, when pressed, they weren't prepared to give him what he wanted. It's a core frustration we deal with on a weekly basis—not everybody gets it.

During the negotiation for Jake's contract, we made our best efforts to convince them of the value Jake would bring to the table, but they simply refused to break with their entrenched employment ideas. In a painful act of self-sabotage, they utterly failed to realize that we are living through a giant sociocultural shift, where the talent has the leverage.

We had better luck convincing the education start-up about Jake. They took him on and accepted his terms because they were on his wavelength; they grasped Jake's cultural orientation and lifestyle choices. They knew he was a true 10xer, which means they understood what kind of growth Jake could bring them.

Today, the pharma firm in question seems to be in a downward spiral—the last of their prior sheen has all but disappeared. Meanwhile, the ed tech start-up that hired Jake has become a market leader in their field. Jake is still one of their regular on-again/off-again consultants, and they know their big, company-wide advances are directly related to the rare level of excellence he and other 10xers like him can provide.

What the losing company had to learn the hard way was this: To attract, motivate, and retain talent in the new workplace, a deeper understanding of the game-changing 10x revolution is now essential.

THE NEED FOR 10x-LEVEL MANAGEMENT

It should be obvious that the world is now tech-dominated, and that puts 10x talent in the driver's seat. What has not yet been absorbed by the powers that be is this: Where there is 10x talent, there is a growing need for a new style of 10x-level management.

Game Changer aims to help redefine the very concepts of talent and management for our new 10x-run world. Through tales from the trenches, we'll explore how the relationship between talent and its proper management is a symbiotic force that can exponentially ensure the greatest chances for sustainable success for all ventures, large and small, public and private. As we will demonstrate, 10x-level management comes in many forms, but it always brings a separate, seasoned point of view, and the ability to see around corners, delivering a critical advantage in an increasingly volatile marketplace. 10x-level management also knows how to spot the instinct for success or sabotage in all prospective clients.

In *Game Changer*, we'll explore a variety of reasons the interplay between talent and management is vital to all of today's workers, no matter their field. Wherever and however you earn your daily bread, office or remote, full-time or part-time, you can frame your job as talent. But in order to become a 10x talent, you must understand how and why strong managerial guidance is essential.

Perhaps the best argument for a rethink of the talent-management relationship is the most obvious one: In your life, you will likely spend an estimated 40 percent of your precious time at work. For better or worse, the talent-management relationship is now one of your closest *personal* relationships, and it has the power to affect your life as deeply as any other.

OUR STORY

Talent is God given. Be humble. Fame is man-given.
Be grateful. Conceit is self-given. Be careful.
—JOHN WOODEN, 1972

Why listen to us? Our breadth of talent management experience grew from a very unusual set of circumstances that nobody could have planned.

In the beginning, we were managers within the music business in the classic mode, and we were quite successful. Our clients included John Mayer, Vanessa Carlton, and other heralded artists. They had hit records, did international tours, won Grammys, and achieved everything a music artist can dream of. We had achieved our dreams, too. Then, without warning, the music industry imploded.

It was not lost on us that technology was the force wreaking havoc on our world.

We knew *we* had to change to thrive, and so we applied our talent management expertise to the tech world, tentatively at first. The results were spectacular, sometimes mind-boggling, and consistently educational. In the first five years, we managed everyone from Google/Apple/Facebook alums to Ivy Leaguers with multiple advanced degrees and veterans of every tech company at the highest level.

It's important to point out that neither of us had a lick of programming experience ourselves. In fact, you probably couldn't have picked two less tech-ready interlopers. We were city kids—byproducts of the hustle-mad New York City of the 1970s. Our paths first crossed at a small Jewish day school in Manhattan. And like many young boys of our generation, we were wildly passionate about music—reading all the liner notes on the LPs, knowing every credit, getting the story behind the story. We went our separate ways after eighth grade—Rishon to the Westside, Michael to the Eastside—but the friendship remained strong through high school. We saw something in each other—the willingness to dream big.

Early on, we both got to view the entertainment business from different angles. Rishon had a close family friend, Dave Hahn, who managed the punk group the Bad Brains. Michael dated Kristen Carr, whose mother Barbara was Bruce Springsteen's co-manager and whose stepfather Dave Marsh is a noted rock critic, historian, and now radio personality. Neither of us knew what we wanted to do exactly, but we knew this: We both had a crazy hunger to build something, to be in the center of things, to *make it happen*.

We jumped at every imaginable endeavor, legal and illegal—everything from the proverbial lemonade stand to fake ID businesses to promoting keg parties in high school. We plotted and schemed, learned the angles: We'd find guys in the city to rent a loft, then we'd strike a deal with the beer distributor and promote the party around to all the private schools and charge to get in—five bucks, ten bucks, whatever the traffic would allow. Some of our early partners in crime have gone on to become successful club owners and restaurateurs.

With each new success or flop, every dicey new endeavor, our hunger grew. We started a T-shirt business, printing them up and distributing them through the NYU dorms. Then, the movie *The Color of Money* came out and we thought, *Why not start our own pool hall?* We raised four hundred grand and scouted a dozen locations—we even considered the notorious, defunct sex club Plato's Retreat in the basement of the Ansonia. The deal fell through—a blessing in disguise—but we kept rolling. Rishon left the city to go to Wharton, the business school at the University of Pennsylvania, and ended up running the concert committee there for three years. Michael went to the University of Connecticut and Baruch College, where he became president of the American Marketing Association. But for both of us, college was the backup plan. We wanted to be where the action was.

In particular, Michael's experiences watching and working with Bruce Springsteen's management team opened our minds to the power of talent management, all that it can be. The relationship between Bruce and his managers had been going strong for almost two decades when we came along. It was a well-oiled machine. The lifestyles of all involved—not just Bruce and the musicians and the managers but the crew and everyone else—were like nothing we'd ever seen anywhere. It wasn't just about the money, the power, the privilege, the comforts of affluence. It was about the *family sense*—the deep mutual respect and gratitude. These were people who were incredibly articulate and not afraid to challenge and help one another. Bruce and his team weren't Us Against the World. They were Us *With* the World.

What we didn't know at the time was that we were beginning our real education in the power of 10x. You might even say Bruce was the first 10xer we saw up close. And the lessons we learned would prove invaluable when we dared to enter the tech landscape.

PLAY FOR KEEPS

In *Game Changer*, we'll juxtapose the worlds of entertainment, tech, megacorporations, start-ups, nonprofits, government, and high finance to reveal how trends are spreading across industries and professions. We'll deliver durable skills and perspectives that anyone who touches the talent economy can apply. And we'll bring firsthand testimony from some real-life Game Changers, everyone from start-up mavens and top show-biz players to blockchain experts, Silicon Valley swashbucklers, and others to whom we've had access from our unique vantage point as tech talent managers.

Our core discoveries may surprise you. Here are just a few in shorthand:

With automation eating up more and more jobs that involve predictable repetition, the new workplace is not a place at all, but a state of workflow that requires far greater flexibility for all parties involved, including openness to third party feedback, group efforts, greater horizontality, greater freedom for the 10xer, and openness to differing generational attitudes.

In the new and utterly revamped work world, tech 10xers control the heart and soul of all businesses, governments, and ventures of every stripe. Don't underestimate their influence.

Great talent becomes 10x when it develops the quality of *manageability*—the ability to seek out and internalize powerful outside guidance, built on an insatiable desire for growth and improvement.

10x managers understand that all talents live on a continuum between Success and Sabotage Impulses—the internal tendency to make positive choices that steer them toward their goals at one end and a denial-based cycle that inadvertently destroys chances for success at the other. The 10x manager knows how to identify the strains and act accordingly.

10x managers must also provide two kinds of Super Vision—Inner Vision, the ability to catch and expose a talent's blind spots and develop strategies to overcome them, and Future Vision, the ability to help talent see around corners.

Not only do all key members of the team need to be 10x and perceive themselves as talents, key members need to also learn how to become strong talent managers themselves, through active practice.

This makes for a Double-Hat World, where talent and management roles switch depending on setting and situation. To cite one simple example, consider a lean start-up where one moment a CTO is writing code and, the next, is managing the team. That flexibility shapes the new world.

Becoming adept at wearing both hats is the surest shot at success in this volatile new work terrain.

Most of all, the talent-management axis requires high EQ, empathy, and the ability to always work with *all* aspects of a talent's life and personality. These strengths always mattered—today, they are nonnegotiable.

This book is divided into two main sections. In the first half, we approach things from the manager's side, exploring all the ways you can attract, develop, and keep 10x talent and make your company itself more 10x. In the second half, we see things from the talent's POV and show how the roles of manager and talent are inextricably linked.

Most important, every step of the way, there are stories and lessons about how you can become 10x yourself. Whether you're a mid- to high-level manager, a CEO, entrepreneur, or a secondary audience of those talents seeking work in the diverse terrain of the modern office, this book will bring you a fresh way of seeing things, as well as practical strategies for success. We have lessons for readers on the tech frontier, but also for anyone interested in the future of work and the nature of success. We have useful advice for those seeking to improve their own path, as well as for those currently involved with STEM both domestically and abroad. On the larger scale, our lessons can help to provide a roadmap for companies, nonprofits, and governments around the globe who want to understand what tactics are required to employ and retain 10xers. And for the individual, we aim to expose aspiring 10xers to the many nuances they'll need to master in order to thrive in an increasingly unfamiliar working world.

Wherever you stand, the game has changed. If you want to be competitive as an entity or as an individual, read on.

GAME
CHANGER

PART ONE

PART ONE

PART ONE

How to Become a 10x Company
and Attract 10x Talent

1 2 3 4 5 6 7 8 9 10

UNDERSTANDING THE 10xer

We shape our tools and then our tools shape us.
—MARSHALL MCLUHAN, 1967

We've told you about how much you need 10xers.

Now we're going to tell you what *they* need.

But before we do, it's important to first understand the terrain. The transformations that 10x tech talent and the new generation of which they are a part have brought to the contemporary workplace are radical and wide-sweeping. They are literally changing the game. We aren't just talking about a mere aesthetic trend or a lateral shift in work processes. This is, in every sense, a revolution. Whoever you are, whatever your gig, the big changes are going to reach you.

It's no accident that the 10x revolution got its first sparks as the curtain dropped on one of America's most tumultuous decades, the 1960s. Upheaval was in the air. In '69, the Stanford Research Institute became one of the four nodes of ARPANET, the government research project that would grow into what we now think of as the internet. The very next year, Xerox opened a Palo Alto-based lab that would go on to create ethernet computing and the graphical user interface. One year later, journalist Don Hoefler titled a three-part report on the semiconductor industry "Silicon Valley, U.S.A." and a new state of mind was born.[1]

The ten years that followed Hoefler's essay make up the decade when most Boomers and children of the '60s got their first taste of grown-up life. In the newly christened Silicon Valley, companies like Atari, Apple, and Oracle all reflected this veer toward the youthful, breeding a unique combo of counterculture ideals, cutting-edge scientific drive, daring technological invention, and strangely enough, the spirit of *fun*—a mix that nobody could have predicted. In hindsight, it's easy to see why the Bay Area, with its long-standing Bohemian tradition and rich academic culture, became the petri dish in which old work modes could not only be mended, they could be countered, ignored, dismantled, and destroyed. The Silicon Valley pioneers were, on the whole, neither business titans whose main motive was profit, nor were they power-hungry builders, driven to see their names across giant monoliths. They weren't even cultural movers and shakers in the usual sense. These were computer geeks— and geeks love doing what they do because *they love doing it*. This key distinction provided the nucleus for a new, interconnected, cooperative, game-loving, data-driven, risk-loving, failure-embracing, fast-minded culture. While nobody was looking, a new breed of talent was born—10xers were coming of age and ready to change everything.

There in the new digital Mecca, far from Port Authority and the traditional pressures of Wall Street, D. C., and the proverbial "home office," the start-up culture was able to gestate outside the public eye with double-speed, giving birth to Cisco ('84), eBay ('95), PayPal ('98), Google ('98), Tesla ('03), Facebook ('04), Uber ('09), and so many more. What's important to understand is that this wasn't *just* a technological renaissance—it was simultaneously a cataclysmic shift in work style and a total attitudinal reset. The acceleration in invention couldn't have happened without a robust disregard for old-fashioned bureaucracies, the norms that used to hold businesses in place. As they digitized the world,

Silicon Valley visionaries also introduced calculated disruption, evidence-based data testing, efficiency adjustments, and, most of all, *a culture of interconnectedness*—advances that have quickly seeped into the broader marketplace.

It's important to acknowledge that technology companies are now taking a beating for everything from fake news to privacy concerns to screen addiction.[2] However, the advances these companies made in working smarter are not in question.

In the beginning, these new work modes barely hung together in what was then uncharted territory. Today, the Silicon Valley way of doing things is a true culture, with its own set of standards and practices. As Steven John, strategic chief information officer of Workday, recently put it: "Silicon Valley is like Tasmania or Madagascar. It's developed different life-forms than anywhere else."[3]

The changes are as deep as they are widespread. In a recent study conducted by Accenture, a multinational company dedicated to the exploration of what they call "market-shaping AI and self-optimizing systems," top researchers looked into what really makes Silicon Valley tick.[4] They identified five unique features of the business culture there that stand apart from its counterparts elsewhere. 1) Silicon Valley is "laid back—but ready for action," with an accent on getting things done quickly rather than agonizing over minutiae. 2) SV players are "committed yet independent," as fiercely loyal to their team as to their employer. 3) This deeply ingrained sense of independence and interdependence leads to an atmosphere that is at once competitive *and* cooperative. It's a unique balance that people from far flung worlds like cutthroat Wall Street or altruistic nonprofits might have trouble understanding. It's "all for one and one for all" but it's also "give me my space." 4) SV employees tend to be both pragmatic and optimistic. And finally, 5) although they are extrinsically motivated, they are *intrinsically fulfilled*. In other words, they see intellectual stimulation, innovation, and problem-solving as their greatest sources of, you guessed it, fun.

Pondering this strange mix, one key stat jumped out at us: 41.6 percent of Silicon Valley engineers contribute to open source code that can be used by anyone for free. If you are not familiar with this concept, open source languages, frameworks, and libraries are ways that software engineers share their work, so that elements can be used over and over by anyone with access to a computer, at absolutely no cost. At the core of this idea is camaraderie and efficiency over money. These mavens would rather donate work for the benefit of saving one another time than get paid for that time. Imagine people in any other industry being willing to share at that level! Even for computer programmers, this figure is more than twice the national average. It's as if Silicon Valley has created a practice of forward-motion cooperation that can be likened to a football team coordinating efforts to get down the field—but all without ever formally defining themselves as a team.

Like we said, they do it because *they love the doing of it*—it's the most important thing you can know about 10xers.

REVOLUTION COAST TO COAST

Today, everyone is feeling the heat from fires those first tech entrepreneurs started. Faster than anyone thought possible, new ways of working have begun to seep into corporate America, with adjustments large and small, ranging from perks like free lunch and snacks to amenities, gyms, coaches, ping pong tables, nap pods, equity, 360 feedback, company retreats, input from everyone, team-building events, meditation rooms, lean start-ups, "move fast or die," the four-hour workweek, acqui-hires, innovator's dilemmas, failing fast, iterating, pivoting, being mission-driven, being data-driven, and much more.

The old-style work culture is toast.

In a May 31, 2019, *Forbes* piece titled "Why Corporate America Finally Embraced Silicon Valley,"[5] Nish Acharya writes that "the realization that start-ups, university researchers, and crowd-sourced solutions can solve certain problems more quickly and cheaply than in-house experts has . . . led a growing number of corporations to adopt open innovation principles." In other words, the very principles that were once exclusive to Silicon Valley. Even behemoths like GM are realizing that the implementation of new technologies cannot only be realized by partnerships with outside start-ups. They're also going to have to deploy new Silicon Valley-style skills training for their staple in-house employees. It's as if David is teaching Goliath how to use the slingshot.

From the outside, some of the aforementioned inventions of the Silicon Valley workplace may look like a soft facade—niceties to make a day at the office seem less grueling. But, in fact, most of these inventions are the by-products of hard data. Placing a nap pod in an office space isn't a lark to grab headlines—it's a move made by smart management who read the extensive research that correlates rest and productivity. Science and those who apply it are driving the game change.

The big companies are taking notes. Some have been plundering the Silicon Valley innovative style by any or all of the following means:

1. Internal Venture Arms, staffed and modeled after independent Venture Capital firms (VC's.)
2. Lab or innovation departments mandated with innovating for the future.
3. Acqui-hiring (also known as Acq-hiring), whereby a company is purchased primarily to recruit its employees rather than its products or services.
4. Partnering with start-ups to foster innovation.
5. Partnering with incubators and accelerators to do the same.

In that same *Forbes* article, John Sculley, infamous former CEO of Apple, emphasizes what he believes are the two basic gifts of Silicon Valley culture: the emphasis on engineering *tools*, in other words, objects that are designed to improve living, and the importance of small teams to achieve "rapid, breakthrough results." Make no mistake, the teams he's talking about are populated with 10xers, and the way they work hard is directly counter to the way many of us think of hard work. What used to be the very image of the serious employee—showing up, putting in long hours, submission to an entrenched hierarchy—is in the process of being utterly revamped.

And the real reason it's being revamped?

So that the 10xers can do what they do best.

SMART FLOW

The first thing 10xers need for you to know is that they are not your every-day employee.

By definition, the 10xer is that rare person with outsized skills, an abnormally positive attitude, and lots of vision, balanced with enough humility to pivot when great advice comes along. When great advice doesn't come organically, the 10xer solicits it, knowing where and how to look for feedback that will help most. Deep curiosity and enthusiasm are always part of the 10xer's game-changing makeup. 10xers often work harder and smarter than everyone else in the room. From their perspective, inefficiency is just a bug they'd love to squash. They see a world filled with opportunities and can move on to the next available one when things don't go their way. They are fundamentally reasonable and willing to accept responsibility for their role in outcomes. In essence, the 10xer alone has the raw materials to go from very good to great to excellent to sublime and beyond.

But they may not operate the way you think they should.

Aaron Sylvan, a CTO-level 10xer who has overseen the creation of many start-ups and raised millions of dollars in funding, says, "Real jobs don't work like homework; the boss can't always control the difficulty." To properly manage a 10x talent, the key is creating a space for them to work smart, on their terms. The real 10xers will solve your problems. Your job is to make the problems clear to them, make sure they have the space, time, and resources to solve them, and then *get out of the way.*

Cal Newport, author and associate professor of computer science at Georgetown University, has coined the term "deep work," which he describes as "professional activities performed in a state of distraction-free concentration that push your cognitive capabilities to their limit." In other words, the kind of work that only 10xers can handle.[6]

With a PhD from MIT, five books to his name, and a gaggle of academic papers and blogs under his belt, Newport knows a thing or two about productivity. (For the record, he's married with two kids and almost never works on weekends.) Newport defines "deep work" as those activities that can "create new value, improve your skills, and are hard to replicate."

What's important to note about Newport's discovery is that it has a grim counterpart, which he calls "shallow work," activities that are not cognitively demanding. This deceptively simple discovery offers what we think might be the starkest lesson for those who balk at the very idea of 10xers: On the whole, Professor Newport notes that shallow work activities "tend not to create new value in the world and are easy to replicate." In other words, if you don't go deep, even work executed by relatively smart, skilled labor won't get you where you need to go.

For those in the know, 10x tech talent are frequently nocturnal creatures and often do their best work, their "deep work," in the wee hours. That's why flexible work hours and work location are important to the 10xer.

Newport's work mirrors what psychologists have long called "the flow state," a term first coined by Mihaly Csikszentmihalyi in 1975 to describe a mental state in which the participant is fully immersed in the act of problem-solving. Along with Jeanne Nakamura, Csíkszentmihalyi defined the following characteristics that make up a powerful mind flow: intense and focused concentration in the present; merging of action and awareness; loss of self-consciousness; a sense of personal control; the distortion of one's subjective experience of time; and last but perhaps most important, a sense that the activity is rewarding.

In a recent CNN Business article titled "These employers don't care where or when you work,"[7] writer Kathryn Vasel explores ROWE, a new company modus operandi that stands for Results Only Work Environment. In a nutshell, ROWE "gives workers complete autonomy, but to be successful, workers need to have clear and detailed goals and metrics." In other words—work anywhere, anytime. Just get the job done right. It's a basic day-to-day policy we've always held here at 10x Management without knowing there was a name for it. As Vasel points out, ascribing to ROWE can be a company-wide management challenge. "It means giving up the deeply ingrained notion that the best employees are the ones who are always at their desks."

Jason Rubenstein, currently CTO of Table.Co and a Python / DevOps maven who has worked as both talent and manager, understands the need for this game-changing freedom. He says he knows a 10xer when he sees one. "They have the personal discipline to sit down and get the work done, *it's a joy to them.* Plus, they always have a subjective level of professional integrity to match their technical ability. I know I can trust them both technically and personally."

A former Google engineer who started programming at age ten by teaching himself FORTRAN at his grade school's lone IBM terminal, Rubenstein has experienced the schism between the old world and the new firsthand. "In the old culture, everyone wanted you in a meeting. And every time you tried to launch a new initiative that involved using remote talent, it was, 'We don't do those things. We *hire* people.' Even now, if I'm working with larger companies, a big part of my job is explaining how the best 10xers work and managing expectations. Some of those companies are *still* so stuck in the old world bottle, I'm talking a 1950s, '60s, '70s model, where you have a CEO completely freaking out, micromanaging the crap out of everyone."

On the frontlines here at 10x Management, we also experience these old world / new world tensions on a daily basis. We can share more stories than we'd like about top-level remote talent who were passed on by the very companies that needed them most, all because these companies held onto the distorted belief that, if they don't see the work being performed in their office, then it's as if it's not happening at all.

As Rubenstein puts it, "They want butts in seats, or at least that's what they *think* they want. What they really want is quality work and real value for their money. Well, how do you define value? It's on us to educate them."

The education process is not always easy and has even been known to backfire. We recently spoke with one prominent manager at a major US bank who told us his board is now reeling back a policy that formerly allowed select top programmers to work offsite. "They're going to start measuring how much time people are in the office and penalizing those who are not," he told us, on the condition of anonymity. We're willing to bet this bank can't pull off their policing effort for long. They need the 10xers more than the 10xers need them. Furthermore, the manner with which they are instituting new policy—without any feedback from their active employees, treating their people like cogs in a machine—runs directly counter to the very game-changing revolution we are describing.

Rubenstein himself says he has mixed feelings about teams being present in the same room. "On the one hand, it's like making music; things do happen when you can see each other. But when you've got serious talent in North Carolina or San Diego, the fact that they're remote can actually be a strong benefit to your team, too, especially if you're working in machine learning, artificial intelligence, blockchain, computer vision—areas where expertise is rare, and working remotely is an aspect of those marketplaces."

On the other side of the coin, in the years that we've managed tech geniuses, we've accumulated countless stories that speak to the enormous benefits reaped by companies that do *not* pass over talent simply because of unusual demands.

In one such instance, a brilliant 10xer we represent named Ryan wanted to be able to work onsite and offsite whenever he desired, and mostly at the hours of his choosing. Ryan was being courted by a best-in-class cybersecurity start-up. His request posed no problem for the company's CEO Arthur who believed that it was better to have Ryan under these conditions than not at all. Arthur knew that putting Ryan's brain power to good use was more important than punching a time clock.

After successfully utilizing Ryan for a number of months, the company ran into a data science problem unrelated to the work that he was doing for them. Still, once he got wind of the problem, our 10xer Ryan was beyond excited about the challenge of taking on a big, hairy, new problem that no one else had yet solved. He was granted permission to work on the issue, and his solution ended up being a game-changer for the company. The result? A radically different valuation for the cybersecurity company on their next round of funding. Just by being flexible and embracing Ryan's demands, Arthur was able to realize value far greater than what he paid.

There's another eye-opening story about the power of 10x flexibility that we love to share with newbies trying to understand the concept. Back in 2017, a thirty-five-year-old freelance software engineer and long-time 10x client named Greg Sadetsky was visiting New York City and sitting in a local internet cafe when Hurricane Harvey ripped into the Gulf of Mexico. As various online communities around the world scrambled to offer the victims assistance, Sadetsky hunkered down and brainstormed new mapping tools to help aggregate information for volunteer rescuers. He wasn't employed by or connected to any formal rescue or weather or environmental association. He was just a concerned citizen. The clock was ticking, and lives were being lost.

As an article by Daniel Terdiman in *Fast Company* describes it, a member of the US Coast Guard named Nathan spotted Sadetsky's map and contacted him. Nathan suggested some new functionalities to assist with the dispatch of helicopter crews. "Over the worst five days of Harvey," Terdiman writes, "the Coast Guard utilized Sadetsky's mapping tools on more than 700 missions that resulted in the rescue of more than 1,700 people, as well as getting urgent medical resources where they were needed."[8] The Coast Guard has subsequently used this software in other disasters.

The 10xers are doing some of the most important work of the twenty-first century, *because they love doing it.*

But they can't do it right if they're hitched to a twentieth-century wagon.

CHARACTERISTICS OF A 10x COMPANY	
0x Company	Allows no remote work and no flex time for people to work off-hours.
5x Company	Is aware that there are productivity increases from better work environments, but still insists on too many meetings, and employs distracting micromanagement.
10x Company	Understands that flow state and deep work trump every other consideration when it comes to productivity. It only requires talent to be involved in essential meetings. Otherwise it lets them do their thing.

EVOLUTION 4-3V3R

Nowadays, the true 10xer can write their own ticket. But just how does a 10xer become 10x? We'll explore this topic more deeply later in Section II, but up front, it's important to accept that the old model of "fixed talent" is kaput. A 10xer, by definition, is not just somebody who can do one thing very well. In these turbulent times, a specialist won't cut it. Tech problems tend to be interdisciplinary in nature, and if you can only do one thing, your value ends when you hit the border of your skills. True 10xers don't hit that border—they plow right on through and keep learning.

Recent studies demonstrate that skills needed for future employment are near impossible to predict because of the rapid rate of change. Adi Gaskell, contributor to *Forbes*, recently declared that "the school ➔ work ➔ retire model is increasingly defunct, and the future will see work and learning blend into one."[9] In what is sometimes referred to as "the fourth industrial revolution," the traditional four-year degree has been debunked for all time in favor of new "knowledge delivery systems" that keep the motivated on the cutting edge, year after year, season after season, even week to week.

One 10xer we spoke to, who wished to remain anonymous, put it like this: "Being too comfortable to a point where you are no longer challenged can now be considered a step backward."

Another 10xer put it this way: "The challenges I love most are doing what seems *undoable*—time-wise, conceptually, and especially technically."

Sam Brotherton is a Harvard-educated 10xer who has handled complex programming for everyone from Whisper and Google to pop star will.i.am. At the time of this writing, Sam eschews full-time employment in favor of heading his own consulting team, and he sees the move toward constant education as integral to the 10x mindset. "It's honestly one of the reasons I enjoy being independent," he explains. "The tech world is evolving really, really quickly. And if you don't constantly evolve yourself, you are going to get left behind. I'm someone who does value being at the cutting edge. I'm currently focused on machine learning and AI, where, in order to stay relevant, you do have to be constantly reading the tech blogs and trying new things. Full-time work with one company can be a problem—it's actually easier to stay abreast of current trends if you're starting a new project every six months."

It's worth noting that Sam works (and educates himself) almost entirely remotely from his home in Salt Lake City. Of his last ten clients, two have been based in Los Angeles, two in San Francisco, two in New York City, one in Switzerland, and one in Chicago. He's only ever had one client from Salt Lake City. "They found me through word of mouth totally unrelated to Utah, and then, when it turned out we were in the same city, we decided to meet up in person just once to close the project. But all the work was remote."

Guessing which subset of master skills are going to be the most valuable next is just that—guessing. The only thing prognosticators seem to agree on is that the ability and desire to learn, change, and evolve at an incredibly fast rate will be *the* crucial components of tomorrow's crop of 10xers. Constant self-evaluation and constant evolution are now the basic survival tools of a radically fluctuating marketplace. Real game changers know how to change themselves most of all.

Paradoxically, although 10xers are paid handsomely, hoarded by Fortune 500 companies, and compared to rock stars and MVPs by the media, one of the first things to go in this new landscape is the myth of the solo maverick, that old cornerstone of the American Dream. The emphasis on teamwork and interconnectedness in tech is so strong that it leaves little room for prima donnas, sometimes referred to as Diva Developers.

"In Start-up Land, highly functional teams are the only way," says Rubenstein, who has been both a top programmer himself and a manager of top programmers. "If you've got someone who isn't really an active member of the team, it's difficult to find out what they're doing because, by definition, there's not a lot of *communication*, right? They have to be particularly mature and communicative to be high-functioning."

We'll talk more in Chapter 9 about the combo of being both talent and manager, and the great gains that come with mastering both roles. For Rubenstein, having to wear two hats has given him unique insight into the art of overseeing 10xers. "I approach my team ready to learn from them, because we're taking a journey together. I've been on their side. I myself was a cocky kid and not easy to manage, and it took a lot of success and failure to get me to professional maturity. Now I understand—a great manager asks you questions, understands who you are. What are your stresses? What keeps you awake at night? Some people need public praise, some can't stand it. Putting yourself in their shoes is the only way to manage a team."

Hero myths notwithstanding, in the twenty-first century, it takes a finely tuned, integrated team with a shared set of goals and beliefs to martial an idea through to success—no exceptions. Sure, Jeff Bezos, Mark Zuckerberg, and Steve Jobs had unique visions, but without being able to incentivize and effectively manage those around them toward cohesive execution, they could not have gotten far. Bezos built his company on what he called the two-pizza team[10]—small groups that two pizzas can feed (ironic since his company would now take about 150,000 pizzas to feed). Steve Jobs famously said that his model for business was the Beatles: "Four guys who kept each other's, kind of, negative tendencies in check . . . the total was greater than the sum of the parts."[11]

For Rubenstein, it's the integration and interconnectedness that we're really talking about. "Teamwork is an actual rubric, right? It's not fifty pairs. It's a concept, but what does that concept really mean? Well—it means communication, daily stand up. Simply put, *conversation*. A lot of soft skills they don't necessarily teach you in programming school."

The 10xer intuitively grasps the importance of the team. Put another way, if you can't evolve with your team, you're just not 10x. In the common parlance, for modern companies to succeed, "the whole team needs to be on the same page," with the same set of overall values and a shared vision for success. A key invention toward this is the OKR (Objectives and Key Results),[12] which has allowed team management and expectation-setting to become less puffery, more science. OKR was first implemented by Intel's Andy Grove in the 1970s but the system has become a staple for many heavy hitters, utilized and popularized by Google, LinkedIn, Intel, Zynga, Sears, Oracle, Twitter, and so many others. It's beautifully simple: three to five high-level Objectives are set up. Objectives should be ambitious, qualitative, time-bound, and actionable by the person or team they're assigned to. Under each Objective there should be three to five measurable Key Results. Each Key Result should be quantifiable, achievable, lead to objective grading, and be difficult, but not impossible. OKR results can be based on growth, performance, or engagement.

The real lesson underlying the growing primacy of OKR in the workplace is not just that objectives and results can and must be measured. It's that accountability is now a shared object for the team. In a stark contrast to old models of ambition and success—think *Mad Men*, or Ayn Rand and *The Fountainhead*—the team now owns invention and disruption, struggle and aspiration, setbacks and breakthroughs. In fact, making it on the team *is* the new success.

It's a tough lesson for some.

Take Brady, a forty-something, certifiable genius. Brady had killer deep-work skills ranging from gaming to mobile, front-end to back-end. He was a fairly early client of ours, one of the first people we took on when we began representing tech talent, and with his set of strengths, his experience, and his gravitas, we were sure he was going to be an amazing resource for the kinds of companies we were talking to. We could envision dozens of work placements where he'd shine.

Sadly, after a few gigs, it became clear that Brady's ability to deal with the companies where we were placing him was weak. He was great—as a solo act—but he didn't play so well with others. His EQ didn't match his IQ. After addressing these issues with him several times, we needed to cut bait. This was a moment we needed to learn to fail fast. We could not take further risks with a 5xer.

Brady was an unusual version of Diva Developer. As popular bloggist and software creator Neil Green puts it, this breed of coder will take any attempt to be managed as an insult. For Green, the average "Diva problem personality is commonly found among long-time developers who were deeply involved in the company's early success. Now, years later, thanks to their long-standing relationships with company founders, they believe they are beyond reproach by a mere middle-manager."

The Diva Dev is the dead opposite of a 10xer, and, of course, everybody knows that these types infect the whole project with low clarity and worse morale. No adaptability means no communication, and that means no 10x results.

On the flip side, we were referred to a younger talent named Katie who had a great attitude and a fairly flexible set of skills. We placed Katie on a gig quickly and when issues arose, she absorbed our coaching and swiftly adapted her work style to incorporate the feedback. Katie continues to thrive in a variety of different consultancies and she uses us liberally to help ensure that small issues don't turn into big ones. In addition to her enormous talent, Katie gets the power of harmonizing with the team. Her EQ and her drive to better understand her own blind spots serve to enhance her exceptional IQ.

Here at home base, Michael himself has begun an annual tradition of requesting anonymous feedback from all the stakeholders in his life, and not just his work life. He solicits candor from family, friends, companies he advises, co-board members, employees who answer to him, clients he serves, coaches, and, of course, his business partner Rishon, his wife, Jenny, and even his teenage kids, Rainen and Lucy.

Of course, some feedback needs to be taken with a grain of salt. The recipient must always evaluate if the person giving feedback has pure motives or if their bias or motivation is causing the feedback to be slanted.

One simple rule of thumb: When someone always gives a certain kind of feedback to everyone they meet, their words can be discounted to some degree. If the criticism sounds way off the mark, checking in with other sources is definitely advised.

All feedback is not created equal.

Still, for the true 10xer, or anybody aspiring to be one, feedback is gold.

CHARACTERISTICS OF THE 10xer

0xer	Gets one degree and thinks he or she is done.
5xer	May pick up skills through work experience, but doesn't go outside for continued education.
10xer	Is not only a lifelong learner, has the grit to face and overcome shortcomings through head-on feedback, which is solicited when it is not proffered.

SURFING THE GENERATIONS

Perhaps the most controversial component of the new workplace is the wide variety of generational differences that coexist on the job today. It's only going to get wilder. No less than 50 percent of the working world will soon be composed of millennials and Generation Zers. Obviously, a smart manager or entrepreneur will learn to communicate with people of all ages, but the newest generations entering the workplace pose particular challenges. They think differently and require different incentives. They've grown up on customized playlists and personalized medicine. Three, four, and five beats away from the twentieth century, their lives have always been digital, always connected. They are the living byproduct of a high tech world—it's no wonder so many 10xers are millennials.

To complicate matters, parents of millennials have instilled in their children that they are uniquely gifted from infancy. They have been told they can achieve anything that they set their minds to. This may not seem like an outrageous claim to them, especially when the most powerful information device in human history can be stuffed into your back pocket.

It's no wonder millennials want to be managed on their own terms.

There's a spate of comical YouTube videos and *Saturday Night Live* skits about this unusual generation. They're easy to make fun of, easy to misunderstand. But all joking aside, those who can facilitate the formidable talents of millennials and Gen Zers will end up winning big. Often-maligned and misread as flakes, millennials are values driven, and if you can find and harness their passion for good, you're in business. Sound familiar? It should—this very quality is often found in 10xers of all ages.

As Anna Liotta, a noted speaker who lectures around the world on generational psychology, puts it, "You are losing talent if you don't know how to lead another generation . . . because they've got options. If what they want to create in their world is not being fulfilled at your organization, they are listening to the invitation from someone else. What they're asking in their heart, in their language is, 'I want to change the world—can I do that from here?'"[13]

We've had our share of run-ins with flighty millennials, but we've also taken tremendous pride in helping a few grow into formidable 10xers. Our colleague Julie Hershman, a New York-based talent agent who has handled musicians, tech geniuses, large events, and more, is a great example. Over the course of five years, Julie went from receptionist to senior management by age twenty-seven—the most reliable person in the room. When she arrived to us fresh out of college, she was quiet. Spookily quiet. The first time we took her out for a drink and got her to speak, Rishon turned to Michael and said, "Oh, that's what Julie sounds like!"

"I couldn't even haggle at a flea market before joining 10x Management," Julie remembers. "The biggest roadblock was dealing with certain customers, specifically older men that thought they knew everything, that were always in the right, and would raise their voices. I had a lot to overcome."

Over just a few years, through patient managerial guidance, Julie emerged from her shell and grew into an assertive powerhouse. She always had the smarts but her power didn't yet have an outlet. We didn't know much about millennials, but instinct told us micromanaging a person of her generation wasn't going to work. Instead, we went counterintuitive, and opted to give her the widest berth possible. We guided by listening. "Rishon and Michael had a very open door policy," Julie says. "And I felt they had a great deal of confidence in me, even as I was just learning."

Since external confidence was the limiting factor, we showered Julie with extra (but legitimate) compliments, promoted her, and increased her responsibilities and her comp before she got a chance to ask. We even pushed her to lead a group in a public setting, difficult but worthwhile. Julie's worth quickly became clear to us and, more important, to her. She now manages other people, software projects, agents of every stripe, and can negotiate with the best of them. In fact, as of this writing, Julie is our lead agent, training newbies and helping to run the show. "Today, I have the ability to negotiate, to handle very complicated customer service issues, to juggle a lot of emails and priorities at once, and to put out fires. I've broadened my skill set and opened my eyes."

It was only by tuning in to the special wavelength of millennials that we were able to help Julie access her strengths. It didn't happen overnight, but once we were able to connect with her desire to help and protect others, Julie moved into the agent role and became like a grizzly overseeing her young, looking after our tech and musical talent. Understanding what was important to her was more than half the battle.

The twenty-first-century workplace may appear a labyrinth to the uninitiated, but it really boils down to openness to third party feedback, group efforts, greater horizontality, greater freedom for the 10xer, and an openness to differing generational attitudes. These takeaways apply to everyone, but younger generations, such as millennials and Gen Zers, have been especially influenced by the radical innovations of 10xers.

Into this new world, the 10x talent enters—as a free agent. To accomplish the unique feat of unheard-of success, they will need strong managerial guidance. In our next chapter, we'll unpack just what great talent management for the 10x age looks like.

CHARACTERISTICS OF A 10x COMPANY

0x Company	Has made no accommodations to understand the generational differences. They expect younger workers, raised in a digital world, to slip into rules and responsibilities that are antiquated and off-putting.
5x Company	Acknowledges generational differences and knows that they need to bend their culture to the new workforce, but they're struggling with how to personalize the environment to the individual when their infrastructure is rigid and brittle and built around the collective.
10x Company	Has implemented OKRs because they know that they need buy-in from everyone. They do quarterly reviews of every employee as well as provide clarity on career path and trajectory. They've also implemented the *why* of their business to their whole team.

TAKEAWAYS FROM CHAPTER 1

- The contemporary workplace is in the middle of a game changing overhaul, a real live revolution, instigated in large part by the spirit of invention that first blossomed in the Silicon Valley in the 1970s.
- Leading the revolution are 10xers, a rare breed of high IQ, high EQ super-talent that have the power to deliver more than ten times expected results. 10xers are natural problem-solvers who do it because they love it.
- 10xers shine when they are given the time and space to enter a flow state of deep work and do what they do best.
- To be 10x requires endless self-analysis, endless self-education, and endless reinvention.
- Teamwork is at the heart of 10x production. So is openness to feedback. The Old School Boss/employee hierarchy is out.
- New, younger generations are bringing a new set of energies to the workplace, many of which mirror that of the 10xer. The smart manager will learn to connect with them as humans and help them harness their enormous powers, recognizing the many places where 10xers specifically and millennials in general share values.

1 **2** 3 4 5 6 7 8 9 10

THE BESPOKE BOSS

I don't think anyone wants to be one of a hundred colors in a box.
—PEGGY OLSEN, *MAD MEN*, 2007

"HAVE IT ON MY DESK BY 3:00 P.M. SHARP!"

Whether you've experienced him firsthand, or you've only heard about him through testimony and tales, you know who we're talking about when we say the phrase *Old School Boss*. (We use the pronouns "he" and "him" because he was usually male, but not always.) This leader of the twentieth-century American workforce didn't have to care too much about the various people who worked for him. In fact, the goals, needs, and personality traits of his team members were mostly perceived as an interruption.

However, the Old School Boss wasn't always merely being a jerk.

He had been given a mission—to put the company first, at all costs.

In the context of his age, it was a system that functioned. If the Old School Boss wanted your report on his desk by 3:00 p.m., he would administer the demand with impunity, and woe to the employee who didn't break a sweat trying to deliver the goods. If the Old School Boss expected you to be present for a dreary, thumb-twirling meeting that had absolutely nothing to do with your actual duties, you showed up with a smile on your face. Most of all, you knew where the Old School Boss stood on your personal aspirations. Without a word on the matter, he assumed you would keep your own desires, dreams, ideas, and expectations in a kind of muted stranglehold while in his presence. You were there to serve him and, by extension, the company, with the same deep sense of self-sacrifice that he did. The trade-off was this: If you kept serving with loyalty and selflessness, the company would keep you employed for the duration of your career, and it might even hand you a gold watch at your retirement party.

In a hilarious but grim article titled "7 Signs Your Boss Is Old School—And How to Deal with It," published on the productivity website Knote,[1] writer Eryn Paul lists a grab bag of red flags indicating that your boss may be a member of what she describes as "The Old Boys Club": He won't allow telecommuting; work/life balance is a foreign concept to him; leaving at 5:00 p.m. is frowned upon; his body language communicates superiority; you're expected to drop what you're doing if called upon, even for superfluous personal requests; taking vacation days, even when you've accrued the time, is an issue; and worst of all, your input is not taken seriously, and when it is, your boss takes credit. Paul concludes by writing that "Old school bosses don't like to change, especially if the change wasn't their idea."

Sound like fun?

The television show *Mad Men* was wildly popular, in part, because it dramatized the very first chinks in the armor of this deeply entrenched style of conducting business, just as the second half of the twentieth century began to dismantle the mores of the first half. Company owners Roger Sterling and Bertram Cooper didn't think of their employees as equals—that notion would have been absurd to them. Even their top talent were expected to behave with a certain amount of deference. Meanwhile, 10xers Don Draper and Peggy Olson saved the company from ruin by employing a modern sensibility and an open-minded work ethic that was foreign to the bosses, and as they won, the balance of power began to shift.

Mad Men beautifully foreshadowed where the modern workplace was headed.

Fifty years later than the era depicted by *Mad Men*, corporate America *still* isn't quite ready to adopt the Silicon Valley's workplace innovations, but increasingly, it has no choice. The millennials have grabbed the ball and they're running with it, drawing from start-up culture, which in many ways acts as a kind of counterculture, redressing staid values. Today, just try barking demands at a 10xer (or any Millennial) and see where it gets you. You might risk undermining your whole company from the ground up. Or try pigeonholing the super talents, and watch your tech bog down and your company crumble as your best and brightest start looking for the exit. In a future that has already arrived, not only can you no longer treat your top talent like cogs—you actually have to have their buy-in for all big decisions that affect them.

In fact, the modern iteration of widely used S.M.A.R.T. goals (Specific, Measurable, Attainable, Relevant, and Time-Bound) helps teams clarify consensus for initiatives. The A in S.M.A.R.T. sometimes stands for "Agreed Upon."

Buy-in isn't required for only short-term project goals. 10xers, like most successful smart people, are forward-looking. As strategic thinkers, they spend a good amount of time focusing and planning ahead. Naturally, one of the topics they have top of mind is where their career is headed. 10xers and millennials need to know that their boss is doing the same, quite literally optimizing their future. Noted generational speaker Anna Liotta calls it a fundamental principle of working with millennials. On her website, she lists it as one of the three mandatory factors in addressing what millennials "want, desire, and in fact demand": *#3 That their BOSS is actively interested in their success and, in fact, is rooting for it.*

Liotta says, "Growing up with coaches, advisors, and mentors as the adult role models in schools, sports teams, and home, millennials are not willing to suffer for eight to twelve hours a day in an authoritarian culture."

Buy-in is the new normal.

So how do you get buy-in and full participation from talented individuals if you can no longer tell them what to do?

The answer is simple: First you have to get to know the Whole Person.

BESPOKE BOSS IN ACTION, PART 1

0x Manager	Barks orders and hopes people will comply.
5x Manager	Considers that people have personal lives.
10x Leader	Knows enough about those personal lives to make considerations when managing them, and in the process, yields superior results.

GETTING TO KNOW THE REAL YOU

The New School Boss puts one question front and center: What truly drives the individual talents at my disposal? How can they be motivated—especially to conquer hurdles that they themselves fear? How can they be helped to achieve project goals from the inside out, in a way that feels natural and holistic to them? It isn't just a matter of incentivizing the top brass. A smart team leader has a vested interest in these questions for every one of their main players. Just as a coach must know their top athletes inside-out, finding the best ways to get the most out of your talent is now the central job of the 10x manager.

The fact is, nowadays you can't even get the 10xers on-board without upholding a custom open-spirited atmosphere. As Dr. John Sullivan at leading recruiting news website ERE[2] recently put it, a majority of companies "don't even know the attraction factors that excite top talent.... If you closely examine your job postings, your careers website, and your recruitment marketing, you will find that in almost all firms they emphasize 'paycheck job' factors like benefits and the skills and capabilities that are needed."

Dr. Sullivan recommends getting past all this, to the heart of what the best candidates really care about—exciting work, a chance to make a difference, rapid growth, and great managers and coworkers. "Assuming the top performers want the same things as the average worker is a common but deadly mistake."

Courting the best tech talent is not different conceptually from getting the best athlete for a pro team. You don't just assess prospects' skills and cut them a check. It's on you to make them feel that they can live the life of their dreams while in your employ. This can never come from a one-size-fits-all offer.

Customization is the new normal.

A-Plan Coaching, an optimized, scalable coaching start-up we advise and participate in, has a rule that we love. When it provides coaching services to a company's employees, they require that the company set a maximum of 60 percent of the employee's goals, while the remaining 40 percent have to be *personally identified* by the employee themself. In order to optimize your workers' work life, you've got to give them the opportunity to optimize their whole life.

It's a level of respect that turns the very concept of *boss* on its head. Your destiny is in your hands, and your buy-in is mandatory. We like this thinking so much that we adopted a version of it, and now, at our own weekly company goal-setting meetings, we ask our employees to set three personal goals for every six professional ones.

Personalization is the new normal.

In fact, with the tech talent we represent, we strive to know them on every level. Our interview process is a sometimes thrilling, sometimes jarring labyrinth, whereby we vet for EQ and problem-solving skills just as vigilantly as for technical savvy. We know, from trial and error, that out there in the real world, the ability to communicate with and relate to others is every bit as important as coding chops, or any other talent for that matter. An A+ developer, engineer, etc. with even B- communication skills will have rough engagements every time.

When we represent executives about to enter a high-level job negotiation as part of our 10x Ascend service, our compensation advisory company, we take our inquiries a step further. One of the first things we do is have prospective clients fill out what we call a Lifestyle Calculator, where they evaluate preferences for themselves (often for the first time) and share with us what is most important in myriad arenas. The Calculator includes twenty-four attributes across which each applicant spreads a hundred points. This very process of self-examination forces prioritization and helps us begin to see who they really are and what is most important to them.

You get to take a firsthand crack at the 10x Lifestyle Calculator here: https://10xascend.com/calculator/. We're willing to bet you learn some new things about yourself. But whether or not you take the tests, what's important to note is that the Lifestyle Calculator reveals time and again is that *no two talents are alike.* A free-spirited, single twenty-seven-year-old engineer is not looking for the same things as a thirty-two-year-old with a spouse and a child. Even two talents who share surface traits often differ wildly in their wants and needs.

The Lifestyle Calculator is just one of a whole flock of new tools cropping up to help managers get to know people beyond their skill sets and work histories. Just as the tech culture is proving to be a game changer for the workplace, new tech itself is now driving a multidirectional renaissance in management tools. *Fortune*[3] recently reported on a giant leap in performance-management system algorithms that are quickly being used by team builders looking to up communication and productivity. As Bryan Hancock, a McKinsey partner in Washington, D. C., puts it,

"Managers and employees alike see the old annual-review approach as too subjective, too bureaucratic, and too backward-looking." These new digital assessment systems deliver up-to-the-minute info about workers, their skills, their goals, and their preferences, so that, as Hancock puts it, managers can concentrate on "coaching people rather than rating them."

Many of these algorithms even make finely tuned recommendations, and if the process sounds like cold data, it isn't. Advice should always be custom, always personalized. Marc Wangel, a twenty-five-year IBM veteran who leads a twelve-person strategy and tech team, says of these new tools: "It actually makes me a better manager. I have more time to meet with my team members for coaching conversations."

Bespoke is the new normal.

BESPOKE BOSS IN ACTION, PART 2

0x Manager:	Gives criticism liberally and rarely balances that criticism with constructive or positive feedback.
5x Manager:	Gives feedback once or twice a year in accordance with HR policies, citing how a worker can do their job better. They occasionally throw in some positive feedback.
10x Leader:	Gives real-time feedback with an emphasis on how the worker can grow and become better at their job and in their career, in addition to formal reviews in accordance with HR policies. They focus on balancing positive and negative feedback at a ratio that makes sense for the individual.

FLEXOLOGY

Nobody understands the fast rate of change in the workplace more than Jesse Lee, an entrepreneur who has spent the last decade reinventing the way brands speak to the young, via his Dub Frequency Media company. Tastemaker mag *LA Canvas*[4] calls Lee "The Magician" and asks readers, "How do you explain how the media mogul handles so many projects without even lifting a finger?" Bloomberg.com is no less wowed—Sheila Marikar's 2017 exposé on Lee is titled "LA's New Hype King Has Cracked How millennials Spend."[5]

Needless to say, Lee is not your Old School Boss.

A young and spirited leader, at turns ebullient and dead serious, Lee dresses in hip-hop high style and runs his buzzing Culver City office with great command. With thirty-five employees between L.A. and New York, and more projects and clients than we can count, Lee has had to learn his management lessons at hyperspeed.

"It's all about finding the right motivation," he explains. "Especially when you're working in a quote unquote 'creative environment'. The only benefit or enticement for strong people to join you is their ability to make an impact. That's what you have to give them."

The key weapon in Lee's arsenal is his ability to create the space for a completely malleable engagement with work. "Two of our newest directors left agencies that work with blue-chip clients to be here, right? Top firms that handle Google, Apple, Nike, to name a few. Because we give them this unique opportunity . . . to *flex,* to do multiple things, in their own way." Lee has also created a practice of finding the right resource for the right job—whether that be a W2 hire or a remote freelancer. He understands that a blended workforce gives his operation a competitive advantage.

Flexibility is the name of the game.

It's a very contemporary way of approaching the daily workload, the polar opposite of specialization. Lee's conglomeration of companies includes everything from red hot PR agency Dub Frequency Media to lifestyle site westwoodwestwood.com to a new high-end retail market-place app, Basic Space. We first met Jesse when he turned to us for a 10x programmer that could manifest Basic Space's enormous potential. At the time, we had no idea how many projects he was juggling. Lee's got his hands in an uncountable number of start-ups, restaurants, and clothing lines. His outfit is especially known for throwing sponsored parties and unusual events, jam-packed with A-list celebs. Lee is the guy Victoria's Secret calls when it wants to make a splash at Coachella.

"Literally, everyone here works on half a dozen to two dozen projects at any given time," he explains. "Imagine a new employee. You go from working on one account at a big agency for two years straight, and then you come here and we get you to help us with Basic Space, with dFm, the tech start-ups, with everything we handle. And we move *really* fast, fast to a point where some people can't handle it. But as a company, we have to flex various muscles at various times, and learn from the mix."

As someone who has cut his teeth marketing to the young, Lee grasps the drive toward personalization as few do. His entire staff is between ages twenty-two and forty, and every two weeks he holds a special workshop for the twenty-seven-and-under set, where they discuss topics of their choice—everything from the art of negotiation to networking, work/life balance, and everyday survival. He also hosts dinners and retreats that place far-flung employees of all levels side by side, just to see what kind of synergy arises. Lee is especially insistent on seeking out the right kind of people to bring onboard.

"When I say I'm looking for a cultural fit," Lee explains, "I'm not talking about the way you dress, the type of music you listen to, external things. *That* stuff is a given, right? I'm also not talking about the skillset and inter-ests that align you with the rest of the team. That's easy enough to figure out, too. What I'm looking for is what I like to call the *growth mindset*."

Lee has pared down this term to represent three factors that he puts in front of any new hire, large or small. Even potential interns have to be scrutinized for the growth mindset. First, he seeks people who are multidimensional thinkers. "When you see a door, what do you do? Do you break it down, kick it open? Or do you go under it, over it? I need people who consider every possibility, who can't just look at a thing for what it usually is. They find strategic solutions from every angle. If you can't do that, then you're the kind of person that gets stuck, and I don't have time to help you when you do."

The second element Lee looks for is creativity, and by creativity he doesn't mean pretty design. "I know a person is creative when they can *make it happen*, get the thing done with no budget and no resources in half the time anybody else would." Juxtapose Lee's statement with the Old School Boss, who would mandate a budget cut and expect the moon from people with no ability to make that happen. By contrast, Lee finds people who will self-impose the biggest challenges, because they have aligned motivation (or what we call *skin in the game*, our subject in Chapter 6). It's another great illustration of how the bespoke boss is always working with the whole person from the inside out.

The last characteristic is the one Lee claims is most important, the one he believes is hardest to teach. "Do you like to exceed your own expectations?" he asks. "Because that's the personality I want working with me—people who want to be successful and perform well for their own reasons."

It's a strong description of what makes 10xers 10x, this drive to exceed expectations and change the game, and you can feel it in the air when walking around the dFm offices. Plain as day, you see the open camaraderie, idea-sharing, and sense of lateral equality that has put the company at the forefront of their field. Lee knows that Old School Bossing just won't play with this crowd, and he constantly works to improve his skills as a leader. He's recently begun a coaching program with Berkeley's resident leadership maven John Danner, and he's enthused about the sessions. One of Danner's practices has been to coach Lee through getting his ideas extrapolated on whiteboard, to connect the dots to convey meaning to his crew.

"John talks to me about being a better translator, right? It's one thing to broadcast a message, another thing to pay attention to whether or not people are understanding it the way I intend."

New School Bosses, if they have the slightest chance at leading 10xers, are as dedicated to self-improvement as they want their team to be. "It's kind of like with coaches and the best players on a team, right?" Lee says. "The best coaches sleep four hours a night, like Bill Belichick or whoever. And then they know that the LeBron Jameses and Kobe Bryants will be out there practicing when nobody else wants to."

BESPOKE BOSS IN ACTION, PART 3

0x Manager:	Wants to do well but only cares about the team as it relates to their own outcome.
5x Manager:	Cares deeply about how the team performs at the job.
10x Leader:	Cares deeply about how the team performs in life and in their career, even beyond the current project or job, often resulting in a team that would follow that leader anywhere and goes above and beyond expectations.

TAKE COMPASSION TO THE BANK

It's no surprise that a digitally charged set of businesses like the kind Jesse Lee runs will tend to gravitate toward bespoke management practices. What's more remarkable is how this new approach is seeping into even the most old guard industries, albeit at a much slower pace. In fact, that slow rate of change is one of the main reasons we wrote this book.

Just like Old School Bosses, old school companies have an uncanny ability to get in their own way. To cite one frustrating example, we recently had to spend more than a month to negotiate a bloated hundred-page master services agreement down to eighteen pages to be able to provide a giant corporation with a seamless conduit to our roster of tech geniuses that they need access to in order to save their hides. Was the agreement really that important to their urgent needs? The hours upon hours of manpower they spent defending it will never surface once our guys get to work. (That said, we give credit to the procurement team at this company for taking the time to trim the fat off the contract. Massive contracts are a major impediment to the ongoing success of a company.)

To cite another, more common example, how come so many companies still have payment terms for individual contractors that are ninety-plus days out? Why would the best and the brightest, who can pull upward of $750 an hour with a flick of the wrist, accept these kinds of terms?

Another example: A forward-thinking executive we work with was recently in the process of setting up a consulting engagement to help a Fortune 100 company be more agile. When they tried to address payment terms in his consulting agreement, they attempted to change the terms to ninety days (their typical pay timeline.) As the executive put it: "That will not work for us. The irony of you hiring me to teach you how to be more agile but telling us that it will take ninety days to pay is distinctly not agile!" The engagement happened with better payment terms.

Fortunately, there are some executives in conventional positions who get that a workplace revolution is underway and unavoidable.

Shelley Seifert, the new CEO of First Bank as of this writing, couldn't run a company more different than Jesse Lee's, and yet she's witnessing the same upheavals and facing some of the same challenges firsthand. As Seifert puts it: "In my lifetime, I've never seen things change so fast. It feels like each season we're at a different level technologically, and the implications are massive."

Started in 1910 with home offices in St. Louis, First Bank is as traditional as it gets, with a hundred-year-plus history of independent, family ownership that uniquely positions it to address the needs and challenges of family owned and other privately held companies. But as the twenty-first century deepens, even First Bank has had to recognize the new state of employer-employee relations.

"Two things keep me up at night," Seifert says. "First is the creation of an infrastructure that supports strong management. And second is the training to make it work. You could have the best, most bespoke manager in the universe, right? But if the system shuts them down in every way, at every turn, then you probably won't keep them for long, because they'll either be pulled to a new environment or get up and choose to go elsewhere. You can't go out and say 'Go ahead and tailor everything' . . . and then the first time you see something that looks funny or new, say, 'Wait, what?' You have to create environments where the change is supported."

Seifert is the epitome of a New School Bespoke Boss, highly tuned to the satisfaction levels of her employees. It isn't easy. Her main accountability is to the board and the shareholders, of course, and her days are slammed with high-level strategy and execution. Still, she makes it a point to meet with the bank's front lines at every level, with special care paid to the tech professionals, from college interns to data security specialists. Often, they're younger and they expect a different kind of stewardship.

"The traditional motivators have changed," Seifert explains, echoing Jesse Lee. "When I entered the workforce, it was, you know, 'How much are you making, can you get a bigger office.' Pretty materialistic. Today, those kinds of incentives just aren't as important. The younger people I deal with are cause-driven, they want to feel part of something. Something that's advancing our environment, something purposeful. Even our deepest tech—they really want to be doing things that help humanity. And you have to address that."

Concurrent with these attitudinal shifts, the banking field now has a whole new level of competition, with personalized banking and fintech services cropping up all over. Seifert says that bankers trained on the twentieth-century model can sometimes be heard lamenting the passing of "the good old days," before every individual expected custom treatment round the clock.

Seifert herself is inspired by the change.

"What I love about the newer generations is that they appreciate local—they go to farmers markets to get value-added advice on vegetables. They don't want or need someone to help them with routine tasks, but they're inherently learners. And these kids are not going to be running family owned businesses in twenty years—they're going to be running things next year. As a bank, how do you help them take those steps?"

Seifert sees a tremendous opportunity to advance the art of management from within this maelstrom of customization. "Whoever manages an individual has a huge impact on their world, so we try to mandate that. We try to hire managers who are open and listen and respond to the needs of individuals. In a perfect world, every manager gets up in the morning and says, 'How can I create an environment where the people who work for me can do their best possible work?'"

This move toward a more holistic style of management is on the verge of becoming ubiquitous in the digital sphere. Jeff Weiner, CEO of LinkedIn, is a vanguard player in the move toward compassionate management. As he recently put it on Oprah's SuperSoul series, "Compassionate leadership begins with the connection between individuals, and a company is comprised of people, that's all it is." Weiner knows that any CEO can pay lip service to humane concepts, but he doesn't believe in empty platitudes. "We're trying to connect with folks, put ourselves in the shoes of others and understand what they're going through, what they're experiencing . . . We're trying to walk the walk."

No surprise that he recently received a 100 percent approval rating from his employees.

100 percent.

This model of compassion at the executive level may be newer for banking than for some other industries, but First Bank's Shelley Seifert embraces it, and wholeheartedly agrees that 10x leadership comes down to a desire to be invested in the fate of others. "It's true that we're asking more of our managers than we used to," she says. "But what's the point of even being a manager if you're not worried about helping others? A manager has to value individuality. It's not about being your worker's best friend, but it's about valuing who they are, and understanding that your job is to support them to be successful. You don't give them anything they want, of course, 'cause that's not gonna help them be successful. But you do work to understand their wants and needs and hopes and dreams as people."

Unsurprisingly, Seifert's bespoke vision sometimes gets snagged by the old system. "The regulatory environment, the whole corporate infrastructure works against the individual, because it's set for a common solution. But that doesn't always lead to the best work. It's not our job to judge what helps a person be the best in their role—we can't be the judge and jury of that. We can only judge the results, and ask, 'What will truly help this person's career?'"

She believes one of the most challenging changes has been cultivating an atmosphere where failure and mistakes can be exposed without negative repercussions—an idea straight out of the Silicon Valley playbook, known best as fail often and fail fast. "If the environment is such that issues can't get escalated, that's a hard fail. And often, an individual who is really good at doing something will try to compensate for issues, to keep them from escalating. A bespoke manager needs an environment where problems come to the surface as fast as possible. You can't fix things you don't know about, and you put the whole company at risk."

In banking culture, creating a sense of freedom for the individual is not the first thing on anybody's agenda, especially at the executive level. "There's a classic problem when great employees, great individual contributors become managers," Seifert explains. "It's like you're a spectacular downhill skier but becoming a manager means having to learn to take a sharp curve. People fall back on what they know and that's dangerous."

And how does Seifert identify the at-risk manager?

"I can see where the major passion is. There are those who are interested in the development of others and those who are really more focused on developing their own careers—a certain rigidity has set in. I look for people who like people."

BESPOKE BOSS IN ACTION, PART 4	
0x Manager:	Wants the work done their way and ASAP.
5x Manager:.	Knows that people sometimes work better under certain work circumstances, with regard to hours and locations.
10x Leader:	Works hard to make sure each person is provided the optimal work environment for productivity.

BESPOKE BOSS IN ACTION, PART 5	
0x Manager:	Worries about their own compensation and only sees the team as a means to that end.
5x Manager:	Gets the team raises at regular intervals.
10x Leader:	Fights like hell to make sure the team feels well taken-care of and explains what he or she can and cannot get for the team and why.

TAKEAWAYS FROM CHAPTER 2

- The Old School Boss, who could make demands of his employees without seeking their buy-in, is a figure of the past.
- The bespoke boss works to understand the whole person—the needs, desires, aspirations, and more.
- This is especially true for bespoke bosses working with 10xers, who require a refined level of focus, flexibility, and understanding.
- New digital tools are helping to advance the management revolution by bringing bespoke, real-time data into the conversation. This advancement is turning the manager into a coach, with a vested interest in each employee's success.
- To reach both 10xers and younger generations, the bespoke boss must appeal to their sense of values and their drive to be a part of some cause that will change the world for the better. In that same vein, employees need to know where their future is in the eyes of their manager.
- Most of all, the bespoke boss requires high EQ and a strong desire to help people achieve what they want, incentivizing from the inside out. Gratitude and compassion are cornerstones of this.
- Overall, to get the best from your team, employees need more coaching and less bossing.

1 2 **3** 4 5 6 7 8 9 10

SUCCESS AND SABOTAGE—
THE MANAGEABILITY CONTINUUM

Addiction, self-sabotage, procrastination, laziness, rage, chronic
fatigue, and depression are all ways that we withhold our full
participation in the program of life we are offered.
—CHARLES EISENSTEIN, 2013

ON THE ARC

In this unruly new work terrain, where bespoke bosses are mandated to deliver customized management for their whole team, one principle stands front and center: You *must* develop an eagle eye for spotting true 10xers. Even the best managers can't deliver 10x results with a weak team. As Michael's father was prone to say, "It is hard to soar like eagles when you work with turkeys."

Very early on in a relationship, strong managers need to understand how others deal with problems, how much responsibility they are willing to take, what truly drives them, and whether or not they are courageous or change-avoidant.

Beyond first impressions and skill tests, a good manager is ready to ask the right questions right away. You can't be afraid to dig deep from the outset, because jerks, bullies, sad sacks, and lazy bums simply *cannot* make the cut, not even for a season. In fact, the vetting is every bit as crucial as the management itself, for even the greatest team leader in the world can't win with talent under the influence of what we call the *Sabotage Impulse*. Of all the things a manager must scan for in a potential hire, be it full-time or freelance, none are as important as this dangerous quality, which lies upon the *Manageability Continuum*.

This Manageability Continuum is an arc that contains a pure, positive drive for individual and collective Success in its healthiest manifestation at one end and a pure, negative, and mostly unconscious drive for Sabotage at the other.

Here's the secret every seasoned manager knows: Even the greatest of raw talents will tend to be dominated by either a Success Impulse or a Sabotage Impulse on the Manageability Continuum.

The *Success Impulse* is the internal tendency to make positive choices that steer talents toward both their goals and the company's goals.

The Sabotage Impulse is a denial-based cycle that inadvertently hurts every last chance for success for oneself and for others. Think shooting oneself in the foot, reloading, and doing it again all day long.

Everyone you meet is somewhere on that arc.

You'll shut me down with a push of your button.
—BEASTIE BOYS, "SABOTAGE," 1994

THE IMPULSES AT WORK

A 0xer driven by the Sabotage Impulse	A 10xer driven by the Success Impulse
Doesn't have a meaningful desire to grow, learn, or evaluate their own behavior. Knows everything he or she thinks is necessary.	Is eager for feedback, learning, and growth.
Will undermine others to save face.	Is not afraid to make changes to themself.
Does not consider others very often.	Wants to support others and shows integrity for their word.
Blames others and tries to deflect responsibility with excuses and rationalizations. Does this both privately and publicly.	Takes responsibility for as much as he or she is responsible.
Doesn't plan much or at all.	Connects values to their work. Is always looking ahead to anticipate and course-correct.
Sees problems as insurmountable and makes excuses.	Sees problems as challenges to overcome and learn from.
Focuses on problems.	Focuses on solutions.
Lacks curiosity and feels he or she knows enough.	Is deeply curious and open-minded.
Thinks he or she is right, even in the face of contradictory data.	Loves data and understands its value.
Communicates poorly, in part because he or she can't think compassionately about the other.	Understands people and knows how to relate and communicate ideas.

A 0xer driven by the Sabotage Impulse (cont.)	A 10xer driven by the Success Impulse (cont.)
Does not have the forethought to see the consequences of their actions.	Uses S.M.A.R.T. goals or the equivalent.
Has no sense or expression of gratitude, and feels very entitled.	Balances ambition and gratitude.
Refuses support and guidance.	Accepts and seeks guidance and help.
Often obfuscates the truth to protect themself.	Balances communication with honesty and diplomacy.
Has an overinflated sense of capabilities, greatly disproportionate to reality.	Knows and respects their limitations.
Creates conflict wherever he or she goes and is perceived as unreasonable by most.	Is reasonable and perceived that way by others.
Is often not happy in or out of work.	Has a work/life balance that brings them some level of joy and satisfaction.
Is lazy and motivated by fear and self-preservation.	Is proactive.
Repeats mistakes because he or she cannot acknowledge any role in them.	Learns from mistakes because he or she owns them.
Often has knee-jerk reactions without considering other perspectives or feelings.	Displays a willingness to try on other perspectives, and pauses before reacting.

THE URGE TO BLOW IT

Never confuse the size of your paycheck
with the size of your talent.
—MARLON BRANDO

The first rule of bespoke management: When you spot the Sabotage Impulse, run like hell.

We aren't speaking hyperbolically. By definition, the Sabotage Impulse eventually sullies every relationship and venture it touches, and it's a strong leader's job to identify it as fast as he or she can, to avoid it when possible, and to flush it out as quickly as possible when all else fails. The Sabotage Impulse can take many forms, and it's very hard to explain what it is in finite terms, but much like pornography or bad advertising, you know it when you see it.

Jonathan Lowenhar is the founder of Enjoy The Work, a successful, San Francisco-based advisory firm that mentors hot start-ups through the thorny thickets of early development. A kind of hands-on, start-up midwife, Enjoy The Work has helped guide birth and growth for dozens of new companies in a wide array of fields, from robotics to finance to AI and beyond, with startups located across the globe, including Mumbai, Toronto, Seattle, New York, Los Angeles, and, of course, Silicon Valley. All this trench time has made Lowenhar a master at spotting the Sabotage Impulse a mile away. He says it can manifest in fledgling start-ups and their CEOs in a number of ways, most dangerously in what he calls The Glass Jaw Syndrome.

"Start-ups are incredibly hard," Lowenhar explains. "You have to move fast or die. It's what makes them a unique asset class and a unique type of entity. Start-ups have limited capital, big enemies, all sorts of pressures, as well as dwindling emotional fumes. For a founder who is paying themself far below market rates while working seventeen hours a day, you've *got* to move fast. In my mind, to pull that off, you have to be rigorously and relentlessly honest about the feedback that's out there. If customers hate your product, if customers like it, if your employee hates it, whatever the feedback is, you've got to be brutally honest about what is really happening *right now*. To pull a phrase from boxing, you'll get knocked out in the first round if you've got a glass jaw. If I can't tell you the truth, no matter how much nonviolent language I use, if I can't have an honest discussion about something that's not working without you personalizing it, without you feeling victimized, then we are nowhere."

Lowenhar is describing a supreme state of unmanageability.

Ironically, Lowenhar was first recommended to us by our former co-founder, as someone who could help us navigate our separation with him. He pulled off this delicate negotiation with such excellence that we decided to continue seeking his advice long after the separation was complete. It's no accident that Lowenhar knew how to finesse a complex breakup—he's fluent in attachment theory. That's why he knows sabotage is going to turn up when he finds a potential client to be trust-avoidant in early meetings.

"One of the first things that I'll look for is how candid, transparent, or vulnerable a potential client is willing to be in those early interactions. If a person is trust-avoidant, they're going to try and test me. They're going to lay little traps. They will be more concerned with being right than finding a real connection. If they're putting up boundaries, they won't feel free to ask questions, and if they're afraid to ask questions, forget it, we can't take them where they need to go."

Lowenhar also cites another fast indicator of the Sabotage Impulse— what his sister Kate has hilariously named the Religious Ostrich Syndrome.

"When things get tough, these CEOs stick their heads in the sand and pray. But start-up life is existential. It means facing tough things. You will face choices that are all suboptimal, and *you will have to choose*. And if you don't? Two weeks later, it all comes back on the table, but now there's that much less time and that much more pressure. Not dealing with what has to be dealt with is one major kind of sabotage."

Chief reality officer is a term Lowenhar has employed to define one of the many hats a start-up CEO must wear. "I don't care if a company has a million people in it or a hundred or six—the CEO has to be able to come in and face those people and say, 'Here's the honest reality of where we are right now, here's what's working, here's what's not working, here's what we are facing, and here's the time we have to address it and the resources available. Let's talk options.'"

Because of the unique nature of Enjoy The Work's mission, bringing rookie companies to market, Lowenhar makes a distinction between sabotage behaviors and a permanent state of sabotage embedded in one's emotional conditioning. "There are bad habits and then there is bad programming." So if you started in a household that was trusting and loving and supportive, you may have grown into an aggressive entrepreneur who sometimes has to act tough and do unpleasant things, but you're still an emotionally healthy human in your core. You've just developed some bad habits to survive. I'll work with that person. But if, in your core, you don't have empathy, if you don't have humility, if you aren't vulnerable enough to hold yourself accountable and learn something new . . . ."

That's sabotage.

Lowenhar goes on to describe meeting a new start-up CEO who was nothing short of a savant. "The processing power in this gentleman's skull was incredible." However, within twenty minutes of sitting down with the alleged super-genius, a half-dozen red flags were raised. "He would talk over us. He would answer his own questions. He repeatedly disappeared into his phone. And every challenge facing the company seemed to be the fault of someone else in the company."

Yet throughout the meeting he would interject, "I really need help, I really need guidance, I'm a first-time CEO." He was well-funded by famous investors. He had a product people liked. He had talented people on the team. But we saw—there's real narcissism here, right? No way can we work with him. You can't coach him, you can't guide him, so why bother? It's not worth your time."

I always had a philosophy which I got from my father.
He used to say, 'Listen. God gave to you the gift to play football.
This is your gift from God. If you take care of your health,
if you are in good shape all the time, with your gift from
God no one will stop you, but you must be prepared.'

—PELÉ, 2006

A TALE OF TWO POP STARS

Can people change? It's the trillion-dollar question.

Just as with the Sabotage Impulse, the Success Impulse may be instantly recognizable to a savvy manager, but we maintain that it also can be cultivated and strengthened when the potential is there. Truly strong management knows when and how to enhance the best qualities already at play, often deploying counterintuitive moves to get a 10x talent to reach for their best.

Our experiences working with pop icon John Mayer provide a textbook example. It should come as no surprise that John was exceptionally smart and hardworking right out of the gate, but so are a lot of people. John achieved great success at a very young age because he could combine all his God-given talent with hard work, drive, and the ability to incorporate managerial guidance. At the time we met him, he was already the poster child for the Success Impulse. He went on to sell eight million records and won multiple Grammys, all before the age of twenty-five, thanks in large part to his ability to not only work hard but to solicit, interpret, and utilize expert advice. He never took anybody's advice blindly. He was diligent in discerning what would serve his goals and what he could ignore.

On the Manageability Continuum, John is at the far end of positive.

At the time we worked with him, he hated international touring. After all, he was already a beloved entity on his home turf. The nonstop promotional requirements of working abroad, with endless repetitive interviews, often marred by journalists asking inane questions, starkly juxtaposed with his US tours where he was already a big star making a lot of money. Asking him to play Europe was like trying to talk him into signing on for a trip to hell. But during one such tour, we got a brainstorm. We decided to take John to meet Bruce Springsteen at his Paris show.

It was a simple move, but sure enough, seeing Bruce command a foreign crowd profoundly helped John understand that skipping all the far-flung places on the globe would be a mistake, one that would be very hard to fix later. John was only able to consider our advice, take it seriously, and change his mind about European touring because he had a double dose of the Success Impulse's most critical quality—manageability.

Following tough advice takes real grit, especially when you're already experiencing some success. It wasn't like the European tours suddenly got easy because John understood their value. Between his natural nocturnal instincts, jetlag, and brutally long days starting with early morning radio/TV interviews and ending with showcases, John displayed his 10xness by sucking it up day after day, night after night, taking care of business across the Continent. Today, he fills arenas in many international territories, long after his initial pop glow has dimmed.

That's what the Success Impulse alone can achieve.

To juxtapose, around the same time, we were working with a client whom we'll call Anthony (not his real name), another supremely gifted singer. The problem wasn't merely that Anthony was not as hardworking as John. The real obstacle was Anthony's low EQ. He had a hard time hearing advice from us or others, and he harbored a deep-hidden resistance to any idea that wasn't his own. Anthony was under the spell of a wicked Sabotage Impulse.

Unfortunately, it took us a long time to see it. We stuck with Anthony for far too long. The problems and pain that caused us were significant. Beyond having invested a lot of time and energy into this guy, we had to reconcile with the fact that we just missed the signs. Problem is, we had a Sabotage Impulse of our own—we wanted to be working with this great singer and performer at all costs. We ignored every red flag with Anthony, chalking it up to youth, praying for a turnaround. Our unspoken fears were proven when, during a TV appearance, he chose to switch songs at the last second without telling anyone, much to the dismay of the host, who introduced the wrong song! This reckless move and its consequences infuriated Anthony's team at the record label, who had spent weeks pushing the very song he refused to perform.

Ultimately the label dropped him. But because we were rookies, it took us even longer to recognize that, no matter how much talent he had, it would never compensate for his Impulse for Sabotage. When Anthony's career started to hit predictable third- and fourth-stage rough patches, we finally parted ways. Among our regrets, we had brought agents, lawyers, and the record label to the table. While they all had the ability to recognize the issues we should have, they went forward with Anthony on our word and reputation. This means we had to live with and learn from not just the damage it caused us, but the damage it caused those who believed in us. This is what it means to live in interdependence.

Looking back, we could kick ourselves for not recognizing where Anthony was headed from the get-go, but that's the conundrum of management: You've got to wrestle down your own Sabotage Impulses before you can spot it in others.

In the years following the loss of John Mayer as a client, we had some very good successes with other clients, but it was all against the backdrop of the recorded music industry collapse. In the ten-year span from 2002–2012, the business went through a massive contraction, physical sales fell off a cliff, record stores closed on a weekly basis, and record labels folded like houses of cards, one after another. The game was changing right under our noses.

The worst part: Our friends were being laid off at labels by the dozens.

To top it all off, the formats of the future were unclear. CDs were a dying beast, individual track sales were never going to catch up, and digital downloads undermined the basic sales format of the industry.

It was disheartening and daunting. We were surviving, but trying to divine the future in the midst of all this disruption and disintermediation was near impossible, both for us and for our Brick Wall clients. We had been doing management for more than a decade by this point, for just about our entire careers. These were dark days, and we were feeling it. Fear and uncertainty were now part of life in a way they never had been before. This was a moment we needed to go back to that entrepreneurial hustler spirit of our youth, and see if we could innovate our way out of the wreckage.

Only we weren't teenagers anymore—we were scared. We both had kids and families. Neither of us had really done anything outside of music, and we had been out on our own for more than a decade. The thought of writing up resumés and getting day jobs was even more frightening—neither of us had been out there in the open market for years.

Michael, being the idea guy between the two of us, went into overdrive. He brought ideas to Rishon, who played the role of devil's advocate, offering healthy skepticism for almost all of them. This certainly kept us from chasing some shiny objects, which would have been bad for us, but it was also a hard dynamic to live through. Making endless suggestions and having them knocked down is no fun for anyone.

Finally, in late 2010, Michael suggested the idea of repping tech talent, an idea that Rishon found hard to poke holes in. We agreed: "Why don't we try it? At this point, we've got almost nothing left to lose."

With that decision, the path to the creation of 10x Management was revealed.

As it turned out, the music industry did right itself over the ensuing decade with the advent of subscription streaming services, so our management company, Brick Wall, did not wither and die as we'd feared. The end result is that we still have a healthy roster of great entertainment clients, and we've also built our tech talent company, 10x, into a meaningful venture.

Yes, we ended up on our feet, but it was a rocky ride and an educational one. Change is possible—but only when you're ready, willing, and able.

Talent without discipline is like an octopus on roller skates.
There's plenty of movement, but you never know if it's
going to be forward, backwards, or sideways.
—H. JACKSON BROWN, JR.

WIN THE TIES

Nobody knows the vicissitudes of success and sabotage like legendary superstar manager Ken Levitan. We've known Ken for years and even had the good fortune of partnering with him on an ambitious indoor drive-in movie theater project called August Moon Drive-In. He has not only made superstars from scratch, he's also saved faltering careers and faced off every hardship of the forever collapsing and reinflating music biz of the New Millennium. As artist manager, career consultant, entertainment lawyer, producer, publisher, restaurateur, and festival owner, he's the last of the great music biz renaissance men, helming the careers of everyone from Kings of Leon, The Fray, Hank Williams, Jr., Richard Thompson, Kid Rock, Alison Krauss, Emmylou Harris, Lynyrd Skynyrd, Trisha Yearwood, Peter Frampton, Meat Loaf, Lyle Lovett, Trace Adkins, Michael McDonald, Ke$ha, and Patty Griffin, just to name a few.

A straight talker with a hardline perspective, Ken Levitan looks for "tie breakers" when considering taking on a new artist. "*Win the ties*, that's my philosophy," he tells us. In a realm where any given radio station can only add fifteen or fewer songs in a week, only a "tie breaker" (aka a 10xer) will go the extra mile and work that much harder to snag the coveted slot.

"First thing I look for," he adds, "is, you know, do they want to do the work. Because we're in a very competitive business, especially for young clients, and no matter how good the music is, if they don't want to do the work, you're already starting with one hand tied behind your back. Newer artists, they're not gonna get paid for two years. And it's hard work. It's a lot of time, and it's time away from family. But you've got to win the ties."

Levitan believes that a strong work ethic is the one aspect of a Success Impulse that no Sabotage Impulse can be allowed to destroy. Nearly a dozen times, he's had to rescue his artists with a drug or alcohol intervention. He's dealt with giant egos who can point to worldwide adulation to back up their every decision. He's even had to deal with clients getting into highly publicized political feuds that alienated a wide swath of their audience. As long as these clients are willing to work hard, Levitan doesn't give up on them.

A master of bespoke management, he compares himself to a chameleon. "You have to get to know them, their family life, their spouses and kids, and everything else. Really, you need to become an extension of their family."

As the founder and co-president of Vector Management in Nashville, Los Angeles, and New York, Levitan doesn't just manage his artists, he manages dozens of managers and support staff, young and old. As with artists, Levitan always scans potential partners for the success and sabotage in their fundamental makeup.

"If a new manager comes in that you like, you don't just look at the depth of knowledge they have in the business. You also have to ask, 'Does this person have the constitution of a person that can really deal with artists?' You have to have a thick skin because artists go off on you. Can you turn them around? Calm them down? Can you make them understand your point of view? What I'm really proud of is not the clients that came out of the box super successful. It's the clients who failed at first, and we hung in there and made success happen. As a manager, you have to be ready to deal with that—you have to not give up. You *will* have failures, and your artists are going to go crazy on you. Can you hang in there and be persistent?"

Levitan's questions are not just relevant for managers and their artists. They represent a set of important questions and feelings that many have about their employees and work teams.

Cheerleader, strategist, chameleon, traffic cop, and aggressively positive life coach—the team leader or manager has to be all these things to channel a super-talent away from Sabotage toward Success.

"I had an act coming back after a big album. I was presenting to their new record company, and everybody was there. Suddenly one of the execs says, 'Yeah, but can these guys still sell any tickets?' I canceled the meeting on the spot. I said, 'Look, if you don't think we can sell tickets, we're done here.' Then I went out and set up a bunch of shows, underplays at three-thousand-seaters in ten to fifteen cities. Because I knew the tickets would sell out in thirteen seconds. And, of course, that turned the people at the label around."

Because Levitan plays both roles, not only managing top artists but also managing a team of managers, his chameleon powers are twice as handy. It's all about bespoke. "In a sense, we've raised a lot of people, because they started here as interns and things like that, and now, twenty years later, we want them to act as strong entrepreneurs. And hopefully they *can*, because they've been trained correctly."

Levitan is reinventing the business by heading one of the first management companies to form its own digital team, tour marketing and band marketing units, and cross-synergizing talents company-wide. Like so many top leaders we spoke with, he regularly holds education seminars for his people, going over the finer points of deal-making, contracts, and relationship-building.

As with Levitan's artists, the work ethic for his managers has to be 10x. "We have a young woman here who, before she went to (music conference and trade show) South by Southwest, she listened to every single demo by every single band that was slated to perform there—almost two thousand acts. That's the persistence I'm looking for. We gave her an easy artist at first, then another, and now, after five or six years, she's starting to become a very successful young manager."

The Sabotage Impulse kills.

The Success Impulse is contagious.

It's one thing to shoot yourself in the foot.
Just don't reload the gun.
—LINDSEY GRAHAM, 2012

THE UP-FRONT NITTY GRITTY

We can't overstate how important it is for bespoke management to determine where a potential client, coworker, investor, or colleague is on the Manageability Continuum, as fast as humanly possible.

The cost of a bad hire is incalculable, and not just from a financial perspective. The crippling effects on company culture and team morale from even one toxic employee can bring a whole operation to its knees. Of course it should go without saying that, during hiring, the chance that you find yourself interfacing with the wrong kinds of candidates skyrockets when recruitment efforts are rushed. Under pressure, companies often hyperfocus on hard skills, asking, "Can this candidate get the job done?" when the real questions should be "Can this candidate get the job done?" *and* "Do they have the necessary Success Impulse to help grow our company culture, plans, mission, and values?"

Skip the second question at your own peril. The cost of a bad hire can be even more devastating to your pocketbook than to team culture. The ripple effects extend further than you might realize. As a recent infographic from Undercover Recruiter[1] explains, your company will feel the financial burn in myriad ways, from hiring and onboarding to compensation to disruption costs to employee mistakes to missed business opportunities and more.

With all of these factors accounted for, Undercover Recruiter estimates that the total cost of *one* bad hire is north of $800,000! And that's just someone who is making an assumed $62,000 a year and leaves after two and a half years. The costs are sure to be much greater for a more senior role.

Now, take that cost and extrapolate the liability for large enterprises—we are talking massive loss. Zappos CEO Tony Hsieh has publicly stated that bad hires have cost his company more than $100 million.[2] That's a heck of a lot of sabotage—though, of course, not all bad hiring is directly related to the sabotage instinct. Still, these chronic bad engagements are just one reason more smart companies are opting to use 10x freelancers and duck the fallout from bad full-time contracts that take time to get into and are difficult to get out of.

Scott Goldsmith is president of Cities and Transit at Intersection, the nation's most formidable smart cities technology and advertising company, responsible for urban digital advertising coast to coast.

As an executive on the front lines of hiring, in a field that can't afford casualties, Goldsmith agrees that a large part of the Success and Sabotage Impulses are inherent. "There are people who are born successes and born saboteurs," he says. "In 10 percent of any group, you have true saboteurs, people who don't hit their goals, people who are *culture killers*, who make everybody miserable, who consistently do things that are questionable for the company. And you've got 10 percent who have a very strong passion for what they do, who are willing to take risks, who have a thirst for knowledge. They're collaborative, they're good culture people. And I can usually tell those two groups within five minutes of the interview."

A graduate of Fordham Law School, Goldsmith has practiced real estate, zoning, and corporate law with extensive experience in land use, historic preservation, and environmental issues. He also serves on the Board of Directors for NYC & Company, the city's primary marketing, tourism, and partnership organization. Goldsmith believes the interview stage is do or die, because the Sabotage Impulse is not that easy to adjust.

"I don't think you can fix a temper. For the bottom 10 percent, sabotage is just so ingrained in their personality. And I'm not a big fan of performance improvement plans. Ninety-five percent of the time, they're not going to make it, and if they do make it, you're just excusing the fact that they're not really the right person for the job because you don't want HR to be upset. It's very unusual for someone from that lower 10 percent or 15 percent to suddenly become a top 10 percent. At best you can move them into the middle group where they can contribute without getting in the way."

Goldsmith is far more optimistic about the 80 percent in the middle, those with mixed impulses. "*They* can change. I've seen examples when great leaders have been put in place that inspire previously unsuccessful teams and individuals. We recently hired a new head of local sales to take over a team that had missed their goals for seven straight quarters. Through a combination of training, team events, encouragement, and a stronger work effort, they've delivered four straight quarters of growth."

Needless to say, impulses don't transform overnight. "The biggest change was . . . the leader worked hard to help the individuals on that team to *change their mindset*. They now have a new sense of confidence." Or, in our parlance, they developed a greater Impulse toward Success.

Still, Goldsmith maintains that if you can nip matters in the bud at the hiring stage, you should. He describes himself as an emotional interviewer rather than a "data guy" and posits that the quality he seeks most in new candidates is a willingness to push themselves harder than any manager could or would.

"I'm always looking for people who think of themselves not as part of the pack but as independent thinkers, willing to challenge the status quo." With this in mind, he's developed an ultra-simple but near-fail-proof technique for getting to the heart of the matter.

"I ask potential new hires one question: *'On a scale of one to ten, how weird are you?'* And I never hire lower than a seven."

Unsurprisingly, the question throws many.

"Some say, *'What do you mean by "weird"?'* Some people say, *'I don't understand the question,'* as in, explain it to me. That's not a good sign."

But Goldsmith believes that those who do answer with confidence tend to reveal something intrinsic about their nature. "The tens, I leave alone, they might be too much to deal with. The wishy-washy answers, the fives and below, those don't really excite me. But the seven, eight, nines—those are the ones I want working for me, the ones who know they think a little differently. I need people in the organization who are creative and smart and willing to be true to themselves like that."

What Goldsmith identifies as "weirdness" may correlate in part with high EQ, the ability to know yourself and identify how you actually feel. Certainly, low EQ is the heart and soul of the Sabotage Impulse. People who don't know how they feel can't stay calm, and people who can't stay calm don't listen to useful advice.

Marc Brackett, founding director of the Yale Center for Emotional Intelligence and a professor at the Yale School of Medicine's Child Study Center, recently put it like this: "The one thing that every CEO of every company should think about is, are the people managing the people in my organization emotionally intelligent and how do the people feel in my organization?"[3]

Feelings may not be what were front and center on an old school manager's mind, but the role they have in discerning manageability today is incalculable. It's important to add that the Manageability Continuum is at play at every stage of a person's career. The Sabotage Impulse can take down a newbie, but it can also make a seasoned player resist management if they aren't careful. There is a phenomenon of Late Stage Sabotage Impulse which sometimes can emerge as a result of success. We have seen people who were great at following advice on their way up but then stopped once they hit certain heights.

We've run into this more times than we'd like to admit. The story almost always plays out the same way. We bring on a new client who's excited and hungry. They then soak up what we hope is good advice which leads them to their first level of success. With musicians in particular, the success comes with lots of people talking in their ears, telling them how incredible they are and how much their music has impacted them. Most of the artists fall into this trap, soak up the adoration, and start to believe that it's *all* of their own making, the power and the glory. Faster than you can say "egomania," they stop listening to their sage advisors who provided the guidance that helped get them where they are in the first place. From there, things instantaneously start to go south.

Typically, one of two things happen: 1) They wake up and realize they're making a mess of what had been working well, or 2) They pick up their blamethrower and begin torching various team members and others for their shortcomings. To wake a talent from egomaniacal slumber in a downward spiral is no mean feat—usually they won't see reality until they hit the ground and it's too late.

On the flipside, some rare talents stay in the game long enough to out-live their initial success. Ken Levitan has a reputation for being especially adept at helping older artists out of late career ruts. He finds that older artists are often more prepared to examine their own blind spots. "It's the ones who have been successful but aren't that successful anymore that re-ally tend to listen, you can sit down and have an honest talk about things. I have one client that would never license their songs—they left millions and millions of dollars on the table. I waited. Finally, when they weren't as in demand, we talked and I said, 'Look, I understand your concerns, but this is one way people will get to hear your music again.' The client came around. They were ready."

A smart, young 10xer on the way up knows that it will take long-term managerial guidance to help them move toward their highest potential and deepest fulfillment.

A seasoned 10xer knows this even more.

They have survived the ugly forces of Sabotage.

THE MANAGEABILITY TEST

Like Scott Goldsmith, when we vet what we think might be a new 10xer, we always ask a series of questions that can point to subtle metrics. The process has shown us just how important it is to understand the various nuances of every person we represent. We love to try and get into the weeds on this, the deeper the better.

Just as with marriage, success is not determined by how well you get along but rather by how well you don't. We want to understand how a 10xer handles tough situations.

Specifically, we hunker down on three areas:

1. How well did the potential 10xer handle a significant mistake of their own making?

    In this question, we are trying to uncover a few things:

    - Do they have an easy time finding an example where they really and truly screwed up, which is, itself, an act of taking responsibility? Or do they spin a story leading to a "soft ending" where they subtly claim it wasn't really their fault?
    - At the time it happened, did they own the *whole* mistake? Or did they try to unload a percentage of the causation to other parties?
    - Did they own the mistake right away? Or did they stall on taking full responsibility, which inevitably makes a bad situation worse?
    - How did they fix the mistake? Were they direct or did they duck and cover?

2. How does the potential 10xer handle a situation where a boss or client wants something he or she thinks is a bad idea?

    Here, we want to uncover the texture of their problem-solving and communication style.

    - Do they start by trying to understand why the boss or client wants to do whatever it is they want to do? Is there a good reason?

- If they don't believe there is a good reason for the request, how do they approach explaining or not explaining why they believe it should be done differently?
- If they are unable to convince the boss or client of their opinion, do they do what is asked, even though they believe it to be an error? Or do they try to explain again in a new and better manner?
- Do they do anything to protect themselves in the event that they have to implement a suboptimal solution? This could be as simple as an email stating, "I am going to build it as requested, but it was important that I document the potential downsides."

3. What does the potential 10xer identify as their biggest professional weaknesses?

    This last one is a deceptively simple question. An answer can tell you so much about the personality before you. Just how credible are the weaknesses they reveal? Just how vulnerable have they allowed themselves to be? Are you dealing with a true 10xer, who strives for self-awareness and can attempt to learn from past shortcomings? Or are you facing someone whose talents and acquired skills have outraced their EQ?

Our interview process includes many other questions but these three, along with a seasoned Spidey sense, can give you a pretty good indication of where someone lies on the Manageability Continuum.

TAKEAWAYS FROM CHAPTER 3

- A great manager spots true 10xers, or those who can become 10x, by looking for where they live on the Manageability Continuum.
- The Manageability Continuum is an arc that starts at Success and ends at Sabotage. Every seasoned manager knows that talent can be ruled by a Success Impulse or a Sabotage Impulse.
- The Success Impulse is the internal tendency to make positive choices that steer a talent toward their goals.
- The Sabotage Impulse is a denial-based cycle that inadvertently hurts chances for success.
- The Sabotage Impulse sullies every relationship and venture it touches. When you spot the Sabotage Impulse, run like hell.
- The Success Impulse may be instantly recognizable but it also can be cultivated and strengthened.
- There is also a Late Stage Sabotage Impulse which can emerge as a result of success.
- Embracing strong management at every stage of one's career is the key manifestation of the Success Impulse.

1 2 3 **4** 5 6 7 8 9 10

SUPER VISIONARIES

I built my talents on the shoulders of someone else's talent.
—MICHAEL JORDAN

So far, we've shown you how the new work terrain has reinvented itself, with 10x talent yielding previously unheard-of power and influence everywhere it counts. We've demonstrated that 10x talent both expects and demands to be treated as whole people, with unique needs, desires, and drives. Moreover, these 10xers know their input is critical to your survival. The sooner you realize you can't live without them, the better.

We've also tried to illustrate how a boss, a hiring agent, or a manager, having discovered what they think may be a 10x talent, must first suss out that person's place on the Manageability Continuum, sniffing for a powerful hidden impulse toward success or sabotage. This drive is most often revealed by that talent's ability to seek out, take in, and utilize credible feedback. In fact, this skill, manageability, is the *ne plus ultra* of what it means to be potential 10x material—no one can be a 10xer without it.

It's a complex set of changes to acclimate to—but all of the above is only the beginning.

Because once a manager-talent relationship is finally in place, that manager must act as no less than a Visionary.

In fact, the manager will need to be what we call a Super Visionary, ready and able to deliver two discrete kinds of Vision that secretly work in tandem:

Future Vision: the ability, when guiding a 10x talent's career, to prognosticate and see around corners, to anticipate dead-ends and express lanes, and to make success happen through strategic and imaginative planning, always conveying that to the talent in a way they can accept, understand, and use it.

And . . .

Inner Vision: the ability to zero in on a 10x talent's blind spots, unknown weaknesses, and misguided drives, giving them a path to improvement that they can understand. Often this involves redirecting focus back to core strengths, always letting a super-talent know when he or she is drifting, getting "cul de sac'd" in rigid behaviors, or "chasing shiny objects."

If Super Vision sounds like a tall order, that's because it is.

Just as the old boss didn't have to care about the real you, the old manager didn't have to care about where you're heading, let alone where you'd like to be heading. Today, whether your talent is an international rock star or a coding maven, a hands-on doer or a superb idea person, it's no longer enough to help them get their next big break or survive their next project.

10xers expect *career sustainability, input escalation*, and *the tools for continuous improvement,* and they will gravitate toward those guiding forces that can bring these things gig after gig, season after season, year after year.

THE START-UP'S CRYSTAL BALL

In Chapter 3, we introduced you to Jonathan Lowenhar, one of the founders of Enjoy The Work, the San Francisco-based company whose very job is to prognosticate outcomes for fledgling start-ups to help them grow without imploding. It's no mean feat, since the rate of self-destruct for new start-ups hovers somewhere close to 100 percent.

Lowenhar knows from Future Vision. His clients are desperate for it.

"The reason these new start-ups turn to us is simple," he explains. "We have seen a ton of use cases. And survived them. And that experience allows us to see forward, where they can't. Here you are, you're a CEO of a brand-new tiny start-up, and you're trying to close your first really big deal. Let's say you're trying to win Amazon as a customer. You've never negotiated with a Fortune 10 company in your life. Well, I have. A lot. A couple of my partners have done it a lot, too. The likelihood that something's going to come up during that nine-month dance that we haven't already seen or can't predict is really low. And I don't care how many books you've read on enterprise selling, we will probably outmaneuver your negotiation tactics all day."

Lowenhar also knows from Inner Vision. His company takes any potential new start-up client through a rigorous "dating period," where they ask tough, sometimes provocative questions, to gauge how well a fledgling CEO can stomach guidance. Enjoy The Work even employs a social-emotional coach to help sift out personality challenges—and blind spots do turn up.

"One of the newer CEOs that we work with, we met when the company was super young, and now they're doing quite well. But we quickly spotted a pattern where this CEO would wake up in the morning, and he'd be angry and he didn't know it, right? He'd come into the office and beat the crap out of the first person he dealt with—you know, emotionally, intellectually, just pounce on the first person that came in front of him. By the end of the day, when his anger would start to wane, he'd take in the breadth of damage he'd done, and he would feel terrible. So he went around apologizing to his people at the end of every day, and they gave him the benefit of the doubt, because they believed he was a good human. They were forgiving, but it wasn't good for morale."

Having recognized a classic Inner Vision sabotage pattern, Lowenhar stepped in to advise. "I had a one-on-one meeting where I said to him,

'Here's the way you're acting. Do you agree? Because this is what I'm see-ing from the outside looking in.'"

In fact, the CEO did agree, but for Lowenhar's cutting-edge bespoke management to work, the conversation could not end there.

"I said, 'My guess is you don't just do it at work. I'm assuming this be-havior shows up in your personal relationships and your romantic ones.' And this CEO was like, 'Yes, wow.' I said, 'You're about to have a child. Do you want this pattern to show up with your child, too?'"

It wasn't an easy discussion to have, but Lowenhar knows that to help navigate business growth, he cannot afford to turn a blind eye to the pre-cognitive psychological conditioning a person has received. What would have been way too uncomfortable for an old school manager—confront-ing the reality of a client's deepest wounds—is mandatory for a bespoke manager in the new terrain. And there are instances where, even the best managers need to call in specialists from the therapy and coaching worlds to help with certain problems that are outside the scope of management.

"The start-up journey is a lonely journey," Lowenhar says. "Everything feels existential. You're just swallowed up by the enormity of the tasks of today, so that it's impossible to think about what's around the corner. But the premise of what Enjoy The Work teaches is that 80 percent of the time, the stages are the same for all start-ups—six stages of maturation."

Those six stages are as follows: 1) defining the customer; 2) product validation; 3) business model development; 4) channel definition; 5) growth; and 6) maturity. It's a complex process, but for our purposes, what's important to note is that Jonathan and Enjoy The Work have de-veloped this pattern recognition to better divine future outcomes.

"If you're honest about what stage you're in," Lowenhar says, "then you can start being honest about where you're headed."

Hustlers of the world, there is one mark
you cannot beat: the mark inside.
—WILLIAM S. BURROUGHS, 1959

THROUGH THE SECOND WINDOW

Future Vision scans the future. Inner Vision scans for the Sabotage Impulse's close cousin, *chronic blind spots*. It's uncanny how these two modes of inspection work together. By bringing to the surface that which the individual talent can't see for themself—their baggage, their obstacles, their misdirected desires and unacknowledged weaknesses—you fortify them for the future when it comes.

For us, one of the blind spots came to light only through the use of our trusted advisor, Jonathan Lowenhar. After years in the music industry where relying on your gut was every bit as important as trying to use data, we were attempting to apply that same methodology to marketing our fledgling technology talent agency. Through a series of carefully constructed conversations where Jonathan was able to point out the weakness and, maybe more important, paint a clear picture of what a data-driven marketing program would look like, we saw the light. It was not easy at first. After all, who wants to abandon their gut feelings particularly since they have been the chief navigation system for almost 20 years. It was a hard realization and even harder to adapt in practice. While we are still getting better at this now, we have come so far and are able to use both lagging and leading indicators to help us navigate these waters and make decisions from a much better vantage.

Here's the most important thing to know about blind spots: Everybody's got them. As Steven Stosny, PhD, puts it in *Psychology Today*, "Our brains are simply not wired for accurate self-evaluation during emotional arousal, which keeps us hyper-focused on possible threats in the environment."[1]

With this in mind, a very savvy manager is attuned to all four quadrants of Johari Window:

1. The Open/Free Area: That which you know about yourself and everyone else knows about you.
2. The Blind Area: That which others know about you and you do not, also known as blind spots.
3. The Hidden Area: That which you know about yourself and no one else knows about you.
4. The Unknown Area: That which no one knows about you including yourself.

Developed by American psychologists Joseph Luft and Harry Ingham in 1955 while researching group dynamics at UCLA, this model was first published in the *Proceedings of the Western Training Laboratory in Group Development*. As website Businessballs.com puts it, "Today the Johari Window model is especially relevant due to modern emphasis on, and influence of, 'soft' skills, behaviour, empathy, cooperation, inter-group development, and interpersonal development."[2]

For our purposes, it's Region 2 of Johari Window that's the kicker, the zone representing ignorance and self-delusion. Region 2 not only represents that which we withhold from ourselves, it also can include that which is being kept from us deliberately by others, sometimes because we unconsciously drive them to keep us in the dark. As Jessica Stillman recently put it in a discussion of Johari Window on Curiosity.com, "Those with an outsized 'blind spots' box may be naive about their own character. They may not see their own aggression or neediness, for example, as clearly as others see it."[3]

When aggression and neediness are present, strong management needs to step in. Like Lowenhar, we have worked with team leaders that don't always treat their people right. One client we love working with is an amazing entrepreneur named Ahmed who oversaw the creation of a multimillion-dollar gaming software. Ahmed is brilliant, charismatic, courageous, and popular—but for all his strengths, he was always getting in his own way, especially at his own company. He took so much pride in the small empire he'd built that his ego was fragile for it, and every time he felt threatened, he'd lash out at those who wanted to help him most, his own team members and co-managers. During more than one disruptive board room argument, Ahmed sounded off like a wounded child. "I invented this @#$%, it's my creation to screw up!"

Slowly but surely, his best people just couldn't be around him. His attitude was his very own kryptonite.

We knew bringing Ahmed's behavior patterns to his attention was going to be painful. As Businessballs.com puts it, "People who are 'thick-skinned' tend to have a large 'blind area.'" That means confronting the blind spots can be more revelatory, more painful, and more destructive. But Ahmed paid for our career advice, it was simply our job, and it had to be done. The question was, did *he* have the fortitude and desire to hear it? One thing we have observed is while the subject often is unaware of the blind spot, when it is presented to them, it is not a complete surprise. For many, they are aware of the impact of that blind spot on their lives but just don't see the behavior itself, and so can't connect it to the results. Given outside perspective, all of a sudden they can say, "So *that's* why these things are always happening to me!"

We had faith in Ahmed. We sat him down and, in the gentlest possible terms, we set up a four-part plan to outgrow destructive behaviors. He knew we weren't crazy. But it's one thing to know you've got to change, another thing to be able to do it.

Like a true 10xer, Ahmed was motivated to grow and, meeting by meeting, day by day, he began not only to treat his people with greater respect, but to understand his place in the scheme of things. He wasn't *just* a brilliant inventor, he was also the recipient of some very fine team support. He wasn't the *entire* "brains of the operation" so much as an integral part.

Most important, he realized in those moments of challenge that people were not questioning him *as a person*. Rather, they were challenging ideas he was presenting. He came to understand (with a little nudging from us) that feedback would always make him and his ideas even stronger.

He also began to understand that if he made it "all about him," he couldn't expect anyone else on the team to be motivated to help build the product. His team would feel belittled and undervalued.

As Ahmed grew, the changes he implemented quickly made way for more and better opportunities for his company. A move toward higher EQ pushed him out of his comfort zone and, as sometimes happens, Ahmed was suddenly, almost mystically rewarded with a major new client—a popular children's property that was a major boon to his business.

The great news is that he knew how to handle it all with grace.

Region 2 of Johari Window isn't always about simple bad behavior. Alexandra Sleator, career coach for Ivy Exec, brilliantly lists "the downside of your strengths" as a prime blind spot for many. "It is about overusing our strengths," she writes. "When we use a strength, things will typically work out. Not only do we do well but it often feels easy because strengths are so natural. All good and well but the risk is to fall into the trap of using a particular strength for all sorts of situations, including those for which it is irrelevant. There is also the risk that the behaviour which uses the strength starts to feel clunky, less fluid; that usually manifest via an energy drain. Using a strength goes from energizing us to draining us. And that's your clue: the change in energy flow."[4] Sleator advises to "dial it down. Moderate its use. Just like good wine!"

One of the key roles a bespoke manager plays is protecting their charge from the burnout that comes from overusing a strength. A wise coach once told us: "If you see someone who is really muscular because they put time in the gym, you'd be impressed by their commitment. However, if they walked around flexing their muscles all the time, you'd be less impressed." A strength is something to deploy when it's really needed.

A great manager uses Future Vision and Inner Vision as twin beams to light the way. They both require a willingness to face negatives head-on. And sometimes, Future Vision is not only about finding out which rainbows lead to pots of gold. Sometimes it means having to protect a 10xer from entering a dangerous neighborhood, or from getting stuck there.

Case in point: We had a tech client placed in a semi-established e-commerce company, and things were humming along. He was building an app, and the company liked the work he was doing well enough.

Still, after twenty years in the business, you get hunches, and our hunch told us things might go sideways.

Signs were subtle, but every time we checked in with the CEO of this firm, he answered our questions in a way that just didn't *feel* right. In fact, today, we can't even recall exactly what set off our Spidey senses. It may have had to do with the way he kept asking for extended payment terms after we had already signed the contract and work was well under way. Or else it may have been his brusque, hurried manner when he spoke to us. Maybe it was neither, but something was amiss.

With this in mind, we called in our client. He told us the app was about half-built. We talked it over, and ultimately we advised him to deliver no more code until they paid him what they owed. We also advised him to demo the work he'd already done, so they could see his progress and get a deeper sense of his value. Show, don't tell.

Our greater thinking was simple: If things go off the rails, we'll at least have a bargaining chip to get him paid.

Sure enough, within two weeks of this meeting, we were informed that the CEO had been arrested—for fraud, no less!

End of assignment.

Yes, our client got what he was owed—but only because we had prepared for disaster by peering into the future and creating extra leverage. "Holding the code hostage" is no way to make friends, but it's a last resort when Future Vision tells you the future looks grim.

FUTURE VISION IN ACTION

0x Management	Doesn't create or look at long-term goals for the team or the individuals on it. Acts and reacts to short-term issues and demands.
5x Management	Has some sense of the goals of employees and has goals for the team. Nudges employees in the right direction when there is an easy and obvious way to do so, but rarely anticipates what is coming to course correct with time and ease.
10x Management	Sits down with individual members of the team and truly understands individual goals—personal and professional, short-term and long-term. Lays out a plan to help team members achieve those goals while ensuring that this plan aligns with organizational goals. Knows where individual and organizational goals deviate and is sure to explain what is and is not achievable for the individual. Always has one eye on the road ahead to alert team members, with as much notice as possible, about possible impending obstacles to their personal or team goals, with an eye on navigation and course correction. Points out to the team member how things align, in order to create intrinsic motivation.

SO YOU WANT TO BE A ROCK STAR?

What used to be truest for show biz, and then for start-ups, is quickly becoming true for all contemporary businesses: The future of any venture is wildly uncertain and the chance for failure is extremely high. Wise guidance is mandatory, and the smart know how to use it.

Quentin Tarantino's *Once Upon a Time in Hollywood* dramatizes client uncertainty in a memorable scene. When silver-tongued talent agent Marvin Schwarz (played by Al Pacino) tells his client, aging TV and movie cowboy Rick Dalton (played by Leonardo DiCaprio) that the future is in Italian Westerns, Dalton is crushed. He doesn't really believe a word of it. All he hears is his own demise. He openly weeps after the meeting and calls himself a has-been. But what the modern audience knows is that Spaghetti Westerns will one day be considered the greatest genre films of their time.

A great manager dares to study the future in ways you aren't ready to explore.

For pop music supermanager Ken Levitan, this ability to predict has to be fortified by real-time flexibility and constant reevaluation.

"Sure, we lay out a plan for the future, and we reason with our artists. Sometimes they agree with that plan, sometimes they don't. Sometimes they're right and you're wrong, they may have a feel for something you don't understand yet. You need a short-term plan and a long-term plan, but most of all you've got to be *nimble*, because all of a sudden something you don't expect pops up. The music business used to be like a children's puzzle, six or seven pieces. Now there's like nine hundred pieces. If, all of a sudden, your act is doing unbelievably well in some random place, you've got to be able to go there and deal with it."

Levitan recounts the meteoric rise of Grammy-winning singer-songwriter Nanci Griffith overseas. "We were trying to build her up in the United States and things were okay. Then she did *one* TV show in Ireland and exploded over there. She became, like, the biggest female artist in Ireland overnight. And that translated into other parts of Europe, where she did really, really well. But we were smart enough to take advantage of it because we were nimble."

In a similar international tale, Levitan tells of Kings of Leon who had signed to RCA Records, only to find weeks later that nearly everybody at the label was about to be fired, including all their major champions. "I said to myself, 'No way (chairman and CEO) Clive Davis is going to understand this band. It's *garage*. And Kings of Leon have this incredible story—their dad was a Pentecostal preacher who got kicked out of the church. But we lost our support at the label, and I didn't know what to do."

On a hunch, Levitan hopped on a plane to the United Kingdom, armed with nothing but a demo and an electronic press kit. He interviewed a phalanx of publicists and hired the best one, and soon Kings of Leon were featured in England's most important music mag, *New Musical Express*, in every issue for the next twelve months, which built them into huge stars outside the United States and set the stage for their eventual US stardom. "Yes, you've got to have strategy," Levitan adds, "but you've also got to be open and alert to *all* your options."

The act of Future Vision is never easy, especially at Levitan's level, where he makes it a point to choose artists who already have a built-in sense of self and a strong sense of artistic mission. "There's definitely conflict. And, you know, at the end of the day, *it's not my career, it's their career*. They only have one career—what happens with it is their choice. Most of all, you've got to make them understand there is an arc to that career. We teach people to be careful money managers early on, to put money away and budget. Because you can't know where things are headed. " Looking ahead is the manager's blackbelt skill.

Sometimes, as with Marvin Schwarz and Rick Dalton, it's all about getting a client to do what he or she does best, but in a new, uncomfortable sphere. "I talked to Kenny Rogers about festivals," Levitan says. "I wanted him to play Bonnaroo. He thought I was crazy. But it ended up being one of the most successful things—fifty thousand people, a young crowd, all singing 'The Gambler.' It was a real moment." It was the beginning of an entirely new chapter of his career that he had long been seeking. Rejuvenated relevance.

To a large degree, Future Vision involves having enough experience and faith to know how certain scenarios are likely to play out.

Then there are those clients, young and old, who "chase shiny objects." In the record biz, that can mean trying too hard to get a radio hit, or chase the newest musical trends at the expense of their musical identity. Sometimes, these artists are being pressed by a record company, which itself is aiming for that elusive overnight killing. Levitan pulls the reins.

"You have to sit your artist down and say, '*Don't do this*. Go with your gut instead. Look ahead. Because you can lose your credibility overnight.'"

A NONPROFIT GAME OF CHESS

No matter your industry, looking forward takes crazy discipline. Like chess, it means meditating on the next half-dozen moves and beyond. By definition, it requires deep education and deeper experience, acknowledging all the while that the game can change at every turn. Newbie small-businesses entrepreneurs and hotshot artists so often don't spend a lot of time growing this difficult aptitude, and that's why they receive the big painful lessons too late. In fact, at its core, seeking managerial guidance is the act of *enlisting experience* to help expose you to your own blind spots and come up with a future plan.

Michael's efforts co-founding and building Musicians On Call—which brings live and recorded music to the bedsides of patients in healthcare facilities across America—has taught us a surprising lesson: Nonprofits are often more adept at strategic planning than their for-profit counterparts. Why? Because nonprofits have no choice but to be disciplined. They have to have a plan, often in order to receive accreditation and funding, and board members and donors want to know what that plan is, in detail, up front. This enforced Future structure keeps all eyes on the future, with a keen sense of survival. For-profit companies are more often judged by present revenue. If that's good, stakeholders can lose sight of the future.

Dr. Jeffrey R. Solomon, former CEO of Andrea and Charles Bronfman Philanthropies (who just happens to be dad to one of the authors of this book) understands the prismatic nature of delivering Future Vision to the board. He has served as exec to many nonprofits and has sat on dozens of nonprofit boards, including the Leichtag Foundation, the Jim Joseph Foundation, the Peaceworks Foundation, and the Diabetes Media Foundation, as well as the city, state, and federal governments of the United States. An adjunct associate professor in the master's and doctorate programs of New York University School of Social Work, Dr. Solomon understands that Future Vision means not just finding but *illustrating* outcomes that clients are not predisposed to have already thought of themselves.

"They may not reward you for telling them what they need to hear," Dr. Solomon says. "I just got off a video call with a program director—I chair his advisory board. During our talk, I helped him see that earned income from fee-for-service sales has greater potential than continuing to rely on donations for virtually 100 percent of his budget. While this man is very talented, a significant pivot like that would not necessarily be on his radar screen."

Insecure 1xers want to be able to say they saw the future themselves. The true 10xer knows that it takes a seasoned outsider who is trained to shoot their gaze forward with sagacious distance to scan for upcoming opportunities.

"Often," Dr. Solomon explains, "management does not really appreciate the value of consultants, board members, coaches, and others who can play this future-seeking role. They think they will be seen as *weaker*, not stronger, for taking good advice. But they're wrong. Wise managers will seek out wise prediction and use it wisely."

Dr. Solomon notes that the need for prediction accelerates alongside everything else in the digital economy. "Five-year plans are less relevant today than they once were," he says. "The world is changing so rapidly, I prefer to think in time segments." He divides the picture into three substantial categories: a) Organizational vision, which is often a twenty-year idealized projection; b) three-to-five-year strategies to help guide the organization, and c) annual operating plans and budgets that reflect the reality of a) and b). "The Future Vision is adjusted in incremental iterations, hopefully always getting better. By the time I or my leadership is addressing the board, I want to have confidence that there is already a shared vision about the future in place."

Just as with the for-profit world, Future Vision must be in natural balance with Inner Vision, and Dr. Solomon has found himself in the uncomfortable position of uncovering the blind spots of board members, managers, and colleagues on more than one occasion.

"One of the finest social entrepreneurs I work with had to be reined in, because, despite the value of his entrepreneurial style, his lack of understanding or accepting the legal and ethical framework of philanthropy got in the way of acceptable behavior. A core principle in my line of work is 'no self-dealing.' There are specific guidelines that prevent an officer or director of a 501(c)(3) (the IRS designation for nonprofit organizations) from using the resources of the charitable enterprise he works for to fund a nonmission-related personal pursuit."

Dr. Solomon goes on to describe an officer who was writing a book and using a colleague as his research assistant. The book was neither in the sweet spot of the organizational mission, nor was it to be owned by the charity. Any advance and related revenues were personal. Solomon had to sit him down.

"The conversation . . . was blunt."

INNER VISION IN ACTION	
0x Management	Doesn't learn much about employees and can't customize processes around the individual.
5x Management	Gets to know employees enough to feel familiar, but not enough to understand what makes them tick. Spots weaknesses and can, on occasion, present them to an individual, but often does so in a clumsy way.
10x Management	Is constantly learning about employees, getting a clear understanding of their motivations, and the full array of their uniqueness (good and bad). Works closely to solicit feedback from employees, with an eye on learning about potential blind spots of team members. Is able to provide insights to the individual employees that are most relevant to their professional and personal growth, with an emphasis on what the employee can't see for themselves. Is able to present these insights to a team member in a way that is always palatable, constructive, and never threatening or punitive, with a singular goal of giving a path to improvement.

When a manager can braid the powers of Future Vision and Inner Vision, honing in on the future while shedding light on the blind spots at home, the 10x talent is empowered as never before. And, of course, 10x managers know that both kinds of vision are always to be framed and presented in a manner that connects with their talent's true personality. Played in tandem, these twin modes are the strongest tools of practice in the art of bespoke management—they have the ability to raise the act of advice-giving to a visionary realm. Suddenly, 10x managers have the powerful tools necessary to course correct themselves and the trajectory of their team or organization.

But none of the great advice that management can provide is worth a nickel if it isn't delivered as part of a genuine interpersonal bond between parties with aligned incentives and a very high degree of trust.

Next chapter, we'll tackle trust head-on.

TAKEAWAYS FROM CHAPTER 4

- Strong management, having acquired a 10x talent, knows it's their duty to deliver Super Vision:
  a. Inner Vision helps talent find and confront their own blind spots.
  b. Future Vision includes predicting short- and long-term outcomes by looking around corners and creating a plan to achieve long-term goals via short-term tactics.
- Super Vision includes keeping clients focused on their core strengths, preventing them from drifting or "chasing shiny objects."
- 10x management makes sure that all this advice and insight is framed and presented in a manner that connects with their talent's true personality.
- 10x management is also attuned to all four quadrants of Johari Window, especially Region 2, the blind spots. The wrong behavior can rapidly devolve into a sabotage pattern that blocks goals.
- Together, Future Vision and Inner Vision constitute the foundation of great advice.

1 2 3 4 **5** 6 7 8 9 10

TO BE GAINED, IT MUST BE EARNED

Earn trust, earn trust, earn trust.
Then you can worry about the rest.
—SETH GODIN, 2014

THE MOST IMPORTANT TWO-WAY STREET IN TOWN

It's one thing to be smart enough and fortunate enough to get a 10xer to join your team. For those 10xers to deliver, however, you'll need to cultivate 10x-level trust. They expect it, and require it. That's because supreme trustworthiness is part of what makes them 10x in the first place. It is also how you move people from being <10x to being 10x.

Unfortunately, trust is as hard to define as it is essential to build. A recent article in *Psychology Today* by Paul Thagard, PhD, posited at least five possible ways of looking at trust: as a set of *behaviors*, as a *belief* in probability, as an *abstract mental attitude*, as a *feeling* of confidence and security, and as a *complex neural process* that binds diverse representations into a semantic pointer that includes emotions. Trust, the article concludes, is rarely absolute, but it usually has an inextricable emotional dimension. "To trust people," Dr. Thagard writes, "you need to feel good about them."[1]

Obviously, developing two-way trust is a cornerstone of any good relationship, but it's especially critical in the trenches of building technology—a messy, complicated process that has a million variables and ever-emerging sinkholes that can derail a project. Those bosses, managers, and team members who can grow a reputation for trustworthiness stand way above the pack.

At the center of workplace trust is a core action from which all trust must grow: expectation management.

> Expectations are a form of first-class truth:
> If people believe it, it's true.
> —BILL GATES

STAND AND DELIVER

As banal as it may sound, whether you're the talent or the manager, the importance of setting and delivering upon expectations cannot be overstated. We aren't just talking about following through on formal agendas. Everything you say, and the way you say it, creates expectations, and those expectations have to be made manifest or there is a price to pay.

This principle is so basic to our view of work life that we hand every new 10x Management client a sixteen-page Best Practices guide that begins with the most important advice we believe we can offer:

"Success is defined by setting clear expectations and meeting or exceeding them. It is that simple."

It's easier said than done, of course, but there's no other way. To make good on your stated intentions is to inspire confidence and rigorous foresight; self-honesty and honest communication must be at play. Every time you present an estimate or a plan, financial or otherwise, and that estimate or plan accurately predicts how reality plays out, you move toward greater and greater trust. It's a commodity that is literally priceless.

Conversely, every time you underestimate or miss the target by creating a false sense of outcomes, you foster some level of doubt, and no matter how miniscule, doubt has a way of growing on itself like fungus. Or, as the old adage goes, "Trust takes years to build, seconds to break, and forever to repair."

Since we are big believers in the value of the lessons learned and growth that occurs from failure, it's important to also acknowledge that, even when you get your estimates wrong, you can salvage trust by proactively and swiftly acknowledging the error, accepting responsibility, and course correcting.

Not long ago, we had two clients working with two different teams within a single medtech start-up. One team handled the firm's front-end development, including client-facing user experience. The other team handled the back-end—the guts of the business. For our two clients, the experiences they had under the same roof could not have been more different.

The back-end development team consistently delivered on budget and ahead of schedule.

The front-end team did not. They had a million excuses, many of which sounded valid and seemed legit, but at the end of the day, an excuse is an excuse.

The people running the front-end team weren't stupid or lazy. The problem was, they were so eager to please that they continued to manufacture or agree to unrealistic estimations, to put the customer at ease and to make management look good.

Our 10x tech talent who had been placed there repeatedly warned his supervisor: "We will not be able to hit these deadlines. We can't build what you're promising as fast as you're promising it. It's just impossible."

Management didn't listen, and sure enough, over time, customers, bosses, and investors were all furious when the team couldn't deliver within the stated timeline and budget.

The back-end team continued to meet expectations and prosper, and our client there stayed on to become a regular consultant and advisor.

The front-end team fell to pieces. In due time, our 10xer said: "I'm outta here. I told them we weren't going to be able to hit those deadlines. They told me to forge ahead anyway, and now they're angry that I didn't do what I said I couldn't do in the first place!"

10xers won't tolerate poor expectation management any more than they'll tolerate getting thrown under the bus for someone else's bad decisions. In a world where they are in demand, they know the 10x skills they bring and the trustworthy manner in which those skills are delivered go hand in hand. And for some 10xers, even when they don't have another option on the table, they won't stay in a toxic situation because they have the foresight to know that no good can come of bad management, either for them or for the organization. They just see a gig with poor expectation-setting as relentlessly pointless.

Smart management also knows the price of untrustworthiness. The cost of missed deadlines, false starts, and blown contracts to the average organization is immeasurable. In fact, it is our belief that being able to find and identify those workers who have a quality of trustworthiness is a big part of what constitutes smart management. We have a saying: "No one is good at estimating technology projects. The only good estimators are those who know precisely how bad at estimating they are."

A 10xer should always review their estimates versus delivery results over time, asking the following: How far off are they, and what was the cause? Without a doubt, patterns will emerge that will help guide you toward more accurate estimations. In simplistic terms, if over time you learn that you are always off in your estimate by a factor of two, all you need to do is multiply your estimate by two and you should be on the money, or at least getting close enough to build trust.

If you can build trust, you can go anywhere.

Distrust all in whom the impulse to punish is powerful.
—FRIEDRICH NIETZSCHE, 1885

PAGING THE FBI

For the 10x talent, a boss you can trust is a rare commodity and a true value when found—a boss who will not throw you under the bus, a boss who grasps your value and your mind, a boss who listens, a boss who gives you the space to allow your talents to work for them. Almost *all* our 10x Management clients (aka the tech talent we represent) complain about micromanagement. They often know more than the people managing them, and there's nothing more frustrating than being paid for your expertise, then not being given the space to allow that expertise to help.

In the fast pace of the modern workplace, how can well-meaning managers, bosses, and team leaders expedite trust building with the 10xers they need most?

An extraordinary article by Thomas Oppong on Medium recently shared "An FBI Behaviour Expert Explains How to Quickly Build Trust with Anyone"[2] from the point of view of FBI behavior expert Robin Dreeke. Dreeke is the founder of People Formula and the former head of the FBI Behavioral Analysis Program, a department whose processes include research into social and evolutionary psychology, honed from years of field experience, and not just any field experience. We're talking about the Federal Bureau of Investigation, an organization that exemplifies the complex, fragile, sometimes inscrutable nature of trust.

In Dreeke's wonderfully titled book *It's Not All About "Me": The Top Ten Techniques for Building Quick Rapport with Anyone*, he uncovers a variety of ways trust can be cultivated on the fly. Some of his ideas are intuitive—eye contact and smiles make for positive, nonverbal communication growers. Some of his ideas are counterintuitive—creating an artificial time constraint can be a positive conversation starter when dealing with a stranger, because it effectively gives them an out. And some of his ideas seem to come from left field but are surprisingly effective in practice—speaking slowly enhances your credibility, because fast-talkers tend to obfuscate.

"Whenever I have a conversation that I believe is important for me to be credible in my content," Dreeke writes, "I purposely slow down the delivery and take pauses for people to absorb the content of what I have just said."

Listening, being curious, asking open-ended questions, and resisting the natural urge to interrupt also make the list, but what is most germane to our vision of trust-building is Dreeke's ultimate call to "suspend your ego." This all-encompassing practice cuts to the essence of communication in the new work terrain.

"Suspending your ego," he writes, "is nothing more complex than putting other individuals' wants, needs, and perceptions of reality ahead of your own."

In other words, when trying to cultivate trust, it's not enough to *act* trustworthy. Real trust is developed in a faster yet deeper and more concrete way when you allow yourself to see and hear and invest your consciousness in the other. To back these ideas up, Oppong quotes a Harvard University research study,[3] which concurs that those who ask more questions, and specifically ask follow-up questions during a conversation, are perceived as more likeable. The empathic communication style cannot help but lead to bespoke management.

One additional surefire means of developing trust that we've encountered is putting the talent's needs first, even when it's counter to your own self-interest. When the advice we are proffering is counter to our own self-interest, we point it out to the talent. Why? Because there is nothing more powerful than knowing a manager is genuinely willing to sacrifice for the talent's best interests.

One of our early 10x Ascend (compensation negotiation) clients had two job offers. Once the negotiation was complete, our client (let's call him Raj) was presented with two options. One company's comp was 5 percent higher than the other, but was going to require that he and his wife move in with his in-laws to make the commute viable. Raj was newly married. The lower of the two packages was near Raj's current home and did not require major lifestyle changes. We advised very strongly that he take the financially inferior offer to preserve the sanctity of his new marriage. What we lost in fees was more than made up for in the trust we gained.

Some great leaders even go so far as to protect their team from blame altogether, knowing that, as managers, all failings ultimately fall on them. This really accelerates the sense of trust from team members.

We had a situation where one of our 10x Management agents made a mistake in negotiating and recording deal terms for one of the freelancers we represent. It was not a huge problem and was easily remedied, but when it came up with the injured party, we took all the responsibility and shielded the agent from any blowback. One might say this is preventing that person from feeling the full brunt of the mistake, but in this instance, we viewed the error as a training failure on our part. By framing it this way, we were able to update our training to avoid future instances, thereby creating an exponential benefit for all future instances. Sometimes you've got to throw out your ego and jump on the grenade.

> You have to trust in something—
> your gut, destiny, life, karma, whatever.
> This approach has never let me down,
> and it has made all the difference in my life.
> —STEVE JOBS, 2005

MEET THE A-TEAM

Nowhere is the crosspollination of so-called soft skills, trust, and tech savvy more apparent than with our friends and colleagues at A-Plan

Coaching, a unique company that is both an affiliation of professional coaches sharing a specific coaching methodology and a bold new smartphone app that keeps clients engaged between sessions, tracks progress, and increases the impact and value of the coaching experience. While we don't envision every manager being a coach, increasingly, savvy managers are employing elements of coaching in their management practices—and seeking coaching themselves.

In a short survey, we asked a dozen of A-Plan's coaches to attempt to define trust for us. Answers were varied and heartfelt: Trust means complete confidentiality; something earned based on an ongoing demonstration of ethics; confidence in the other person's integrity; a safe place for vulnerability; a zone where access to the truth can unfold; the freedom to be yourself and know it will be received and reciprocated.

The coaches also explored "trust fails"—times when coach/client confidence got breached. One coach expressed that "trust goes off the rails when people are scared or feel judged. That's when they tend to lie in order to avoid the truth, when they deceive to protect themselves, and lack progress forward because the safety to explore is no longer there." Another coach noted that trust falls apart "if the principles of appreciation, gratitude, and encouragement have veered too far off track." A third, discussing the challenge of trusting her teenage son, wrote that "he has a high level of integrity, but his honesty is compromised when he needs to protect himself."

One thing they all agreed on: When trust waivers, empathy can go a long way toward course correction.

A-Plan's co-founder and CEO Sara Ellis Conant is a pioneer in the coaching field, with more than twenty years of experience, an MBA from Stanford, and coaching engagements everywhere from Google and the City of San Francisco to Pfizer and Yesware, among others. A frank and engaging speaker, Conant believes there are no shortcuts. The seeds of trust must be planted through listening and commitment, and first impressions are key.

"At A-Plan, we have a very specific structure for how our coaching relationship begins," she explains. "During the first call, the coach mostly does the listening. Simply listening is the single biggest move toward trust. It's such a rare gift to receive in our society, to be well-heard, to not be interrupted, to not have someone interject with 'Oh yeah, me too, I had that same experience' or 'Here's my advice on that.' It's so rare to not have somebody be corrective or contradictory—especially if people are expressing upset."

A-Plan's second call, or the *launch call* as they refer to it, involves the coach immediately making a series of firm commitments—to complete confidentiality and to the preservation of a judgment-free zone, where emotional expression is welcome but never demanded. The effects are instantaneous.

"When I make that commitment and ask for a new client's commitment in return, I am also explicitly asking for them to trust me and trust the coaching process," Conant says. She also asks new clients to only be completely candid when they want to be, and to be unafraid about telling her what topics are off-limits. "When people know they have a choice, when they don't feel forced, trust follows."

In a very contemporary parallel, the open-minded coaching approach that Conant brings to A-Plan is matched by the "blue sky" business savvy of her co-founder, Michael Counts, a User Experience expert and immersive theater artist with credits and accolades in mobile tech, live entertainment, tourism, opera and live concert experiences, transportive experiences, and the application of emerging technologies to all of the above.

For Counts, the coaching experience is invaluable precisely because deep trust is at play.

"There's a layer of trust with great coaches and managers that goes beyond basic alignment," Counts says. "With those guides that have meant the most to me, there's always a kind of *spiritual trust* that impacts the relationship. I almost want to say the trust has to go beyond the relationship . . . both parties have to have a trust in the universe. As in, 'I trust that the universe has brought us together.' Both parties have to be willing to lean into that and see where it leads."

Counts is the very picture of an idea man, and he's been responsible for a variety of wild productions, from a live immersive experience based on and in partnership with *The Walking Dead* to an elaborate video installation at Lake Nona, Florida, to a $12 million, one-night Michael Kors launch party in Shanghai. Getting guidance for his one-of-a-kind career can be a challenge.

"A great coach doesn't rubber stamp you. They are never business as usual. They ask tough questions in an empathic way. And I'm one of those people with a refined authenticity detector—it picks up little things about someone over the course of time. What motivates them? How do they treat others? How do they handle setbacks? When I'm dealing with an authentic coach, I know it because I feel it."

This feeling isn't just a phantom. As Counts explains, neuroscience tells us that fear and resistance create a chemical reaction that quite literally pushes us into our amygdala—the fight, flight, or freeze mode. Acts of spiritual trust, as he defines them, are those shared behaviors that gently move us back into our prefrontal cortex, the command center that plans complex cognitive behavior, personality expression, decision-making, and social behavior. "That's where creativity happens, where innovation happens. Our deepest levels of communication and spiritual awareness are there, waiting to be tapped. A great coach, a great manager can take us there."

Trust is like the air we breathe—when it's present,
nobody really notices; when it's absent, everybody notices.
—WARREN BUFFETT

EMPATHY, VULNERABILITY, DIVERSITY, FAMILY

Most people have a sixth sense for what's fair, no matter what their stated moral and ethical beliefs are. That's why the boss who blames everybody on his team cannot ultimately be trusted. It's simple cause-effect: The boss looking for a scapegoat will not have a team willing to take risks. The boss who insists that you stay in your lane even when it's not logical will not get your valuable input. People put on the defensive cannot shine, because the defensive position does not foster trust.

Most of all, it's very hard to trust those who cannot expose their own shortcomings.

Conversely, bosses who are human, fallible, responsible, and directly vulnerable are people for whom you want to deliver, not because they pay you more, not because they are your best friend, but because they exhibit the qualities of a *worthy, responsive human capable of exchange.* They show you *their* humanity through vulnerability, and they recognize *your* humanity through empathy. Most of all, the good boss takes responsibility right away. In fact, taking complete responsibility for managerial actions and shortcomings is a crucial way to engender trust.

The trust bond energizes, motivates, solidifies.

It works.

The opposite of trust is blame, which creates a culture of ducking and covering, just as in the story we told earlier in this chapter. Somehow people seem to think that if you don't blame, you can't hold people accountable, but this could not be further from the truth. Blame makes people feel *less* accountable.

Interlaced with this need for workplace trust is the need for diversity—a hot topic in any era, and one that has reached a fever pitch in the last decade. Why are trust and diversity so tightly bound? Because for diverse groups to actually function together, they must stand on a bedrock of communication and trust.

In interview after interview, the top managers we spoke with noted that one of their most critical, long-standing goals is creating an environment where people feel safe enough to express diverse and divergent ideas. The Old School Boss didn't care about such things.

It should go without saying that the corollary to this is creating an environment that allows for diversity of the team members themselves. When we speak of diverse teams, we are talking about a range of ages, genders, religions, races, sexual orientation, identity, and ideology. There are many volumes written about why having diverse teams is better for all outcomes, so we won't spend a lot of time validating what should be obvious, but it's worth noting that, where trust is concerned, diversity presents special challenges.

In order to best succeed when you have diverse teams, you need to create enough shared trust so that you can actually benefit from that diversity. The most mixed team in the world is static if people don't feel safe enough to express alternate viewpoints. In particular, if a manager or leader doesn't value the full range of perspectives, their people will not be forthcoming.

The irony of this is that virtually every corporation in the country is actively trying to improve their diversity stats for a variety of reasons. Some want better optics. Some want to be perceived as being more politically correct. Some have heard that, statistically, diversity delivers better outcomes. These companies are spending so much time and energy bringing diversity in the door—which is great—but getting everyone to have a seat at the table is only half the battle. They need those voices at the table to be able to speak up. This can only come from trust.

Oftentimes, establishing real trust in a diverse environment means getting past surface words, to reach what a team player really means. You can never listen closely enough, and parsing words from intentions, and intentions from words is one of the cornerstones of our art. When one of our very successful music clients said, "I don't want to do that Broadway show," we knew that really meant, "I don't want to do that Broadway show for that long." Just as "I can't deliver that user interface" may mean "I can't deliver that user interface in the way you're asking for it." But you have to know your client well enough to dig out the truth under the words. Michael jokingly calls this ManageMeant, the ability to parse what is said versus the true message.

For example, we had a brilliant gig for one of our best programmers, Monica, and we couldn't wait to pitch it to her. The job seemed to meet all her criteria, and yet she declined. She said it just wasn't for her, but because we sensed something peculiar about her rejection of the assignment and because we had built up a sufficient level of trust in our relationship with her, we could sit down with Monica and discuss the why of it. We discovered that she was concerned about being embedded in the all-male *brogrammer*-culture of this particular company. A brogrammer, for those not familiar, is defined as a male computer programmer who engages in stereotypically male-oriented activities and macho behavior. (Sorry to report, it's very popular among fast growing start-ups as well as larger corporations, as documented in Emily Chang's harrowing *Brotopia: Breaking up the Boys' Club of Silicon Valley*.)

Once the issue was on the table, we were much better able to address it, first by creating a trial period for the engagement to see if the fit would be okay, then by coaching and empowering her to set boundaries so that her voice would be heard. Monica went on to be one of the most respected members of that team. She also ended up really liking the gig and extending her time there more than once.

It's a great example of why diversity should not be framed as altruism. From a business perspective, hiring Monica was strategically the best move they could make—she's amazing at what she does. That team almost missed out on a truly fantastic developer who brought a totally different sensibility to the project. The great irony is that her presence was doubly important, since the audience for the product they were developing was more female than male.

Whatever the culture of your team, if you haven't protected and promoted the value of diversity and divergent thinking, you're losing some of your best assets. On countless occasions, we've asked our own staff to help us see things through *their* lenses. Some are millennials, some are female, some come from very different worlds than we do. We've discovered that by creating this trusting environment, people put forth ideas that are very different than our own, often leading us in important, unexpected directions. We had one instance where we were planning to name a particular group activity *Netflix and chill*, a phrase one of us overheard at a cocktail party. At the time, we didn't know this was a pop-culture reference for sex. Had younger team members not pointed this out to us, we would have created a tremendously embarrassing situation for ourselves. This is a miniscule example, but imagine if Chevrolet had a Spanish speaker in the room when they were naming the Chevy Nova? They might have chosen a different name since that literally means *Doesn't Go* in Spanish.

In the next section, we're going to switch POVs and explore how the individual can become 10x.

And when we say the individual, we mean you.

THE TRUST MATRIX	
The 0x Manager	Doesn't really care about trust. Assumes their charges will follow management directives no matter what; confuses authority with leadership.
The 5x Manager	Understands that trust needs to be built up, but assumes that will happen on its own, over time.
The 10x Manager	Knows that the development of trust is a two-way street. Knows that it's incumbent on them to set and deliver on promises. Knows that the manager must get to know the professional goals of the talent. Knows that it's on the manager to proactively advance those goals. Knows the biggest way to achieve all of the above is by doing something for the talent that is not in the manager's own self-interest.

TAKEAWAYS FROM CHAPTER 5

- Trust is difficult to define but essential to build for all smart managers and all 10x talent.
- The cornerstone of trustworthiness is setting, communicating, and delivering upon valid expectations.
- When you find yourself unable to deliver upon expectations, owning your error quickly and course correcting are essential. No one is right 100 percent of the time, but you can be honest 100 percent of the time.
- There are a number of methods to help expedite the building of trust, but none is greater than "suspending your ego" and learning to listen deeply to the person across the table.
- In addition to listening, trust is built upon a foundation of honoring commitments, especially the commitment to be present.
- Empathy and vulnerability enhance trust by letting us know we are connecting to a fallible human with the integrity to be honest even when it is hard. Especially when it is hard.
- Diversity and trust are intertwined. Diversity without trust leads to a stultifying atmosphere where people are afraid to voice their different but potentially beneficial opinions.

PARTTWO
PARTTWO
PARTTWO

How You Can Become 10x

Yesterday I was clever so I wanted to change the world.
Today I am wise so I am changing myself.
—RUMI, THIRTEENTH CENTURY

PREAMBLE: CHANGING HATS

In the previous chapters, we've tried to demonstrate the radical effect 10x talent is having on the workplace. We've also shared some critical lessons for management when trying to identify, procure, develop, manage, and retain that 10x talent.

For the next five chapters, we're going to switch gears and approach this new equation from the talent's side.

Just who do we mean when we say the word *talent*? In our worldview, everyone can frame themselves as talent, and everyone can strive to be 10x. Without a doubt, that includes you. Everyone can strive to become more 10x, and that means moving from average to good to great and even to exceptional.

Of course, a true 10xer is a rare animal, a mixture of staggering intellectual capacity mixed with rare emotional sophistication, and not everyone can or will get there. Still, in these next chapters, we will share those critical elements that a large swath of talent *can* attain to help push them down the path toward 10xness.

It's also important to note that these upcoming chapters are not just for the talent. Embedded in each lesson are prime directives and perspectives for the management side. Ultimately, we aim to prove that talent and management are yin and yang, interlocked and inseparable, each containing the essence of the other, sometimes even within a single person.

If you think this next section doesn't apply to you, keep reading.

1 2 3 4 5 **6** 7 8 9 10

SKIN IN THE GAME

If you've got a talent, protect it.
—JIM CARREY

Most self-help and get-success books orient themselves by placing the reader (i.e., "the talent") at the center of the discussion: their skills, history, personality. *"It'll all come to you, if only you prime yourself properly for the right breaks."* Fair enough.

But we see things differently.

We know that for 10x talent to thrive in this new unwieldy environment, they are going to need the guidance of someone else: a seasoned, reflective, intermediary force with a separate POV and what we call "skin in the game."

When we say "skin in the game," we aren't just talking about a percentage of earnings.

Skin in the game means way more than financial stakes.

It means emotional and even spiritual stakes.

It means belief.

Strong management that has a vested interest in your success must always be dedicated to your cause, beyond percentages and hyperbole. Your win is their win, and vice versa, at the deepest life levels.

To reiterate, we use the phrase "management" in this book to denote any number of relationships—the word could signify a manager in your organization on whose team you work; it could mean an outside entity with skin in the game who is helping you navigate your career; it could be a leader in your industry with whom you have struck up a mentor/mentee relationship. Whatever the set-up, skin in the game is mandatory. They have to know that your success is their success, too.

In fact, as far as we're concerned, for any form of management to even be strong, it has to be willing to go to the mat and kill (or die trying) for their talent. The half-invested aren't worth your precious time.

This skin in the game is an important asset for talent at every stage of their career, because strong management is the only force that can bring the benefits of experience to bear on your maiden voyages. In other words, what a talent is going through for the first time is often something that strong management has dealt with and refined their approach to, situation after situation, year after year.

Even more important, strong management with skin in the game is frequently the only outside entity that can deliver unbiased (or, at the very least, less biased) advice toward aligned interests. If there is one thing the great managers have in common, it's their embrace of the unvarnished truth.

This is why, for fledgling and experienced talent alike, it takes guts to be managed. You've got to be ready to take advice that is sometimes counterintuitive, sometimes hard to hear. Inevitably, managerial advice is most valuable when it's hardest to hear.

Letting another person help guide your destiny is nothing less than an act of faith.

Skin in the game is what delivers that faith.

WHAT TO DO WHEN YOUR BOSS IS THE BOSS

In order to illustrate skin in the game, we went straight to the top. Nowhere is the utility of this force more evident than in the decades-long, multitiered relationship between supermanager Jon Landau and his most famous client, Bruce Springsteen.

If there were ever two guys who might be described as game changers, Landau and Springsteen are them.

In '74, Springsteen was just an up-and-coming artist with a few noteworthy records and no hits to his name. Landau, a respected, pioneering rock critic, had the audacity to write, "I saw rock and roll future and its name is Bruce Springsteen." This bold statement was the first of its kind and was Jon's first example of putting skin in Springsteen's game. He literally would be wrong if Springsteen failed, and therefore it was now in Jon's interest to see the opposite occur.

Springsteen was flattered, of course, and the two struck up a friendship. In those embryonic days of the rock press, the division between artist and critic was not so very wide, and camaraderie of this kind was not completely unusual. What was unusual, however, was just how much they hit it off.

Within months, Landau switched gears and became Springsteen's producer on nothing less than his breakout album, *Born to Run*, considered to be one of the greatest rock LPs of all time. (Unless you've been living on the moon since August 1975, you probably already knew that.) When Springsteen had a falling out with his then-manager, he and Landau decided to work together as artist and manager, and the rest is rock-and-roll history. For almost half a century, they've been thick as thieves, demonstrating the highest level of shared skin in the game—artistic, financial, emotional, and spiritual alignment.

How did it happen?

"When it comes to artists," Landau told us, "if you *love what they're doing*, they can feel it. And that's a good starting place."

Unsurprisingly, Jon Landau is a larger-than-life personality himself, with enough great anecdotes and tales for ten books. Still, looking back on those early days, he's both candid and discerning, and even a little awe-struck himself.

"The way I describe it is, we were sort of dancing around each other. I'd written about him, and that was an important review for him, of course, but we had no formal relationship whatsoever.

"So one day he calls me and he says, 'Jon, why don't you come down to Long Branch tonight' over in New Jersey where he was living. He says, 'Let's hang out and listen to music, I got some records here, and let's just keep talking.' And I say, 'Sounds like fun.' But lo and behold, there was a huge snowstorm that night, and I mean *huge*. Roads are blocked, it's a mess. So I call him back with the assumption that, you know, we'll postpone.

"But Bruce wasn't really a realistic-type person. He wasn't interested in the weather. He was interested in doing what he wanted to do. And what he wanted was to stick to our plan. I was about to explain that the roads were closed and so forth, but I could tell . . . he really wanted me to visit. So, I said, 'Bruce, I'll be there.' I had no idea how I'd get there.

"It turned out that *some* trains were running, but completely off schedule. I seem to remember getting a ticket and leaving at around 6:00 p.m. and arriving somewhere around midnight. A six-hour train ride to Long Branch! Bruce's place was right near the train station. I don't remember if I just walked there in the blizzard or what.

"We spent all night talking, until 8:00 or 9:00 in the morning. I said, 'Bruce, I gotta go home. This has been great but...I gotta get some sleep.' Well, he checked and the roads had cleared, so he showed me the best way home on the bus."

At this point in telling us the story, Landau pauses. He seems to be shuffling through a thick deck of vague memories and lost notions, detours and paths not taken.

"Now, you know," he says, "I don't know if that's why I became the producer of *Born to Run* and Bruce's manager. But I have the feeling—I have always had this feeling—that if I hadn't gone there that night . . . it wouldn't have happened."

What we glean from this awesome story is a lesson for every aspiring talent and every manager out there: Going out on a limb and demonstrating real skin in the game, especially without an agenda, is the truest—no, the *only*—way to build a credible talent-management bond.

Landau is quick to point out that he and Bruce don't usually deal in role titles like "manager" or "producer." But when the Boss lost his manager and was unsatisfied with working through entertainment lawyers, he knew he needed someone with skin in the game to represent him.

As Landau explains: "Record companies don't want to deal with an artist that wants to manage himself. If the artist starts calling up direct, asking, 'Why am I not making the Billboard charts?' it's very uncomfortable. You have to have kid gloves on when you're talking to the talent, and it's stifling.

"From the other side, the artist also can't say 'Screw you' to the record company and get into a big fight about some important things the way a manager can."

A rapidly rising star with a full-throttle work ethic and a schedule to match, Bruce turned to the person he related to best—Landau.

"We had a six-month trial period. I told Bruce right off that I had no business background at all. I didn't know anything about it. He said: 'You're a smart guy. This other stuff, I get the feeling it's not rocket science. And we trust each other, that's the important part.'"

Landau jumped into the deep end, handling all aspects of Bruce's career and enlisting the best in the biz to educate him wherever he needed guidance.

For contracts, he called on David Geffen. "I learned so much about management from David," Landau says. "The way he would agitate for artists he believed in. The way he wouldn't take no for an answer. The way he would never quit. Also, he had this belief in quality, especially about people. Everybody associated with him was the best at what they did."

Over time, guys like Geffen and Landau helped reshape the spirit of rock-and-roll management—from cigar-chomping loudmouths exploiting and sometimes even bullying their own people to serious representatives who respect their artists and defend their talent to the world. Landau told us that in forty-five years, he and Springsteen have raised voices to each other maybe three times. Yet an ongoing dialogue and very open communication is the key to their bond.

"In the early years," Landau explains, "we were looking to be perfect, and one of us would get onto an idea that the other didn't see, and we didn't know how to *close* it. But since we've gotten older, we've learned how to bounce ideas and let go. You have to learn where to stop. You have to learn to grow up."

What's also striking is that, forty-five years down the line, Landau still takes enormous pride in what he contributes to Bruce's career in the present.

"The show went on at 8:00," he says, recounting a concert challenge. "I watched the first hour, a big outdoor show. Then we went down to catering, which was near enough to the stage that we could hear the show. I'm standing there with George Travis, Bruce's long-time tour director for almost as long as I've been with him, and Barbara Carr, the partner in my management company. All of a sudden, the sound cuts out. I say, 'George, what's happening?!' Well, as you can imagine, we went flying out of our seats.

"It turns out that the primary generator had gone south. It was like the show stopped dead. Oh my God, never had anything like that happened. We had a safety generator, and we scrambled to hook it up. Finally, we get things humming, and Bruce *works twice as hard*. The crowd got as good a show as he could do that night.

"Show's over, Bruce is walking down a ramp, and I'm standing on the ramp, and George is with me. And to our amazement, Bruce is . . . ecstatic. Because the show has ended on a high. He looks at us, and he says, 'Gentlemen, there's only one thing I want to hear.' Well, George, God bless him, starts explaining in detail what happened with the generators. I grabbed his arm and said, 'George, I'll take it from here.' Bruce wasn't in-terested in the details. I knew what he wanted to know right then and there, so I looked Bruce in the eye. 'Bruce, that will never happen again.' Of course, Bruce, George, and I knew that no one could literally promise it would never happen again…but that was the closure that was needed right at that moment."

The reason Bruce Springsteen could take Landau at his word is because of half a century of skin in the game.

> The energy you create around you is
> perhaps going to be the most important attribute.
> In the long run, EQ trumps IQ. Without being a source
> of energy for others, very little can be accomplished.
> —SATYA NADELLA

WHAT'S REALLY AT STAKE

Sometimes skin in the game doesn't come from a single individual. Just as Springsteen went out on a limb when he saw 10x qualities in Jon Landau, Landau himself knew he had met his 10x business partner for life when he connected with Barbara Carr, a legend in the world of rock music. "Couldn't get along without you, Barb," is the way the Boss put it to the crowd on the night he was inducted into the Rock and Roll Hall of Fame.

Barbara Carr knows a thing or two about talent and management.

A student of Marymount College and the London School of Econom-ics and a former publicist at Atlantic Records, Carr has a reputation for being capital-T Tough, a formidable gatekeeper who is incredibly orga-nized and smart and suffers no fools. Before joining the Springsteen camp, she was already widely credited with having created tour publicity, whereby music artists interface with local media as they make their way around the globe. A simple and logical concept, but like many great ideas, no one before Barbara had the Future Vision to see it. She literally changed the game.

Today, Carr herself travels with Springsteen on most dates of every tour. She also leads his considerable charity efforts and is a trustee of The Kristen Ann Carr Fund for sarcoma research, named for her daughter who died from the disease in 1993 at age twenty-one. As of this writing, The Kristen Ann Carr Fund has raised more than $23 million since its inception in 1993.

And to what does Barbara Carr attribute the incredible success and remarkable longevity of her team?

"We manage each other," she says, with an infectious laugh. "We're very respectful, very careful with each other, because everyone has their ups and downs, their good days and their bad. It's like family. It's about staying calm, having some humility and some perspective and also just really keeping in mind that everybody involved is a human."

The record biz was very much a boys' club when Carr got started, and she can still recall earning $5 an hour at Atlantic in the 1970s—any number of small-minded guys wanted to take her job or see her fail. As the first woman to become head of a department at a major record company, she cracked the glass ceiling for several generations that followed, and stood her ground with some of the most feared characters in show biz. Today a powerhouse manager in her own right, Carr forms an interesting equation when describing the formidable managers and execs she's worked for and worked with over the years, from Landau to the infamous Atlantic Records founder Ahmet Ertegun to the legendary former Sony Music Entertainment boss Tommy Mottola and beyond.

"The reason these people are known for having a large leadership aspect, the reason they can wield power so well . . . is because of their *passion*. Yes, they are managers, but they're really artists themselves, they have an artistic part of them that is undeniable. Look at Ahmet. The story goes that he got started selling records out of the back of his car. He's an artist, in that he's a visionary. Jann Wenner had a vision when he started *Rolling Stone*. Jon Landau certainly always had a vision for Bruce, though perhaps he wouldn't put it that way. But these guys were visionary and artistic themselves, and that's why they could lead artists."

This, for our money, is one of the best descriptions of the yin-yang nature of talent and management. Great managers have skin in the game because management itself is their art, their talent.

Their own vision is part of what's at stake.

Smart 10x talent can spot that key difference a mile away.

For Carr, this vision must combine with a genuine emotional attachment to the talent's work for management to be truly effective. At a recent screening of Springsteen's new documentary, *Western Stars*, she burst into tears.

"I was crying so much at the end that I could barely tell Bruce what I thought of the movie. I just got moved, totally. You know, all of us are getting older, Bruce just turned seventy, and the movie makes you think: I am going to stop and smell the roses, I am not going to sweat the small stuff and care who left their shoes in the middle of the kitchen or whatever. You know—*I am capable of change*."

She pauses to reflect, and adds, "How can I ever retire? Why would I retire from this deep emotional experience? I'm so proud to take this to the rest of the world."

Recounting all this to us, Carr cried a little again and tried to apologize, but we understood where she was coming from. She has the deep sense of connection great management always has to the talent and their work. That heart-and-soul connection is what's at stake when we say *skin in the game*.

After a sigh, Carr captured the nuance of this talent-management yin-yang even more succinctly. "It's like . . . we're managing Bruce . . . but there's a way that you might even say he's managing us right back . . . through his inspiration."

*One of my greatest talents is recognizing talent
in others and giving them the forum to shine.*
—TORY BURCH

DISTORTION, REVERB, AND TONE

Skin in the game isn't just the glue that holds rock stars and their superstar managers together. It's a state of affairs without which no business can function. Wherever you work, in order to be 10x, you need your boss or manager or team leader to understand that you're hitched together, that you share fates.

As we've noted, this means keeping an open mind even when the guidance isn't attractive at first glance. After all, what talent in their right mind would listen to someone advising them to turn down millions of dollars for a few months of easy work, in order to go lose money on something more difficult that might pay long-term dividends? Smart talent would, if they knew their advisor had real skin in the game. As you learned in Chapter 3, John Mayer did—because that's what smart talent does.

In fact, convincing talent to make counterintuitive career moves is a major part of our job, and it's only possible once they know that we sink or swim together.

Our tech clients, for instance, often look to us to advise on which engagement is right for them when they have to choose between two, three, or even four active offers. In one such instance, a coder named Aviva was looking at two opportunities that both had appeal, but one was offering a much better rate. Despite our own desire to make the bigger commission, we advised Aviva against taking the higher paying gig because the founder doing the hiring seemed like an egomaniac and our Spidey senses were on high alert.

Aviva resisted our advice at first—she really liked the idea of the better rate, not just for the money but because it would have been the most she had ever made, a symbolic win.

She said, "Are you guys sure you aren't leading me away from my big break?"

We had to remind Aviva that our advice was not mere opposition—we would be making less money, too. We said, "The only possible reason we would guide you like this is for better long-term benefits . . . for you and for us."

She got it: Our wagons were hitched.

We recently looked into the company that had offered Aviva a higher offer, and it is no more. We certainly don't get it right every time, but this was a corner so easy to see around, it was practically transparent.

As we said, it takes guts to be managed, and not everybody has the stomach to embrace it with the same gusto. It's a practice, and a practice takes practice.

Gary was co-founder of one of the top ten websites in the world when he came to us seeking management. We were happy to take him on as a client, but we soon learned that Gary could be paranoid in unpredictable ways. Right out of the gate, every piece of advice seemed to put him on the defensive, and even after we secured him his first two stellar engagements, he was ready to walk because it took us a bit too long to find those first gigs for him. Despite our business model really aligning with our client's interests (we earn a percentage of the client's revenue), he still was sure there was some angle. It was only through careful explanation that there was no way we could win without him winning that we got things back on track. Of course, this was a sign of trouble to come, but he was quite exceptional and worth the time and attention. More than once, we had to talk him off the ledge. Despite the fact that he was making more than he had before and getting more praise than he had before, he tended to equate input with hostility. It was chronic.

One of Gary's customers was paying him quite well, but would make requests that really pushed his buttons, and after a couple behind-the-scenes meltdowns, we knew we needed to intervene. We came up with a plan. We taught Gary to come to us first when something got him riled up.

We convinced him to:

1. Vent to us.
2. Take time to adjust to the new information.
3. See things from the other side.
4. Let us play bad cop when needed.

One of the methods we have employed to help Gary sounds comical but it's darn effective: Whenever Gary gets particularly sore about an email he's received, we have him read it out loud, with several different vocal intonations. Read it once as though it was angry. Now read it as though it was super matter of fact. By doing this he is able to see how he inserts his own feelings and ideas on to words that may or may not have included those feelings. This simple ritual has made it very clear to him that he is not always right about what he thinks he hears, or, to put it more accurately, he is always interpreting matters in a subjective way—it's in the nature of being human. Getting in touch with his own subjectivity has allowed Gary to make small perceptual shifts, in order to interpret (in fact, reinterpret) input differently (i.e., maybe they are not angry). Overall, we have found this to be a great technique in helping our clients and team parse what is there from what they think is there.

None of the above would have worked had Gary not developed a sense of our skin in the game first. The most important thing we taught him along the way is that there is really no way for us to exploit or take advantage of him without shooting ourselves in the foot.

MOMAGERS, SPOUSAGERS, FRIENDAGERS, AND OTHERS

Who has skin in the game in your life?

In the entertainment world, it's not uncommon to have a family member, spouse, or friend in one's corner, especially in the early days of one's career. In the professional world, it's equally prevalent to find a mentor or coach through existing connections—someone who can help guide at the personal level.

Because of the premium placed on trust and familiarity when skin in the game is at play in a manager-client setting, it makes a certain amount of sense to seek advice and guidance from those closest to you. Having a momager (a mom who is acting as your manager) has many benefits. After all, who wants to see you succeed more than your own mother? Spousagers and friendagers can sometimes get in on the act, too. What good friend wouldn't want to help you when asked? In some cases you may not have another option, so asking those closest to you for advice and guidance may seem like a better option than going it alone.

Still, there are a few obvious pitfalls to be aware of when enlisting the near and dear. For starters, every industry has its standards and practices. If your momager isn't familiar with industry norms, she may suggest things that are way out of step. We always joke that if you showed a non-entertainment attorney the best record deal that has ever been done with a record company, they would advise their client not to sign it because the terms are so bad. Furthermore, simply wanting the best for someone isn't exactly a credential, so the Third Party Effect, which we'll talk about in Chapter 7, is weakened.

We heard a story, hopefully an urban legend, about a Millennial writer who misspelled a word and, when her editor corrected it, she told her editor that that's how *she* spelled the word. When the editor insisted that the word be fixed, the writer called her momager from the office to scold the editor.

In a hilarious Fox News piece titled "Entertainment pros: Most Hollywood moms should be moms, not momagers,"[1] writer Hollie McKay points out the inherent conflict of interest in momagering. "Wanting what's best for your kid, but also wanting what pays the most for you—that makes being a momager way too risky a proposition." Cautionary tales include Brooke Shields's mom, Teri, urging her minor daughter to appear nude in a role as a child prostitute, and R&B crooner Usher being forced to fire his momager, Jonetta Patton, for "different view and mind-set." Ariel Winter, of television's *Modern Family*, fired her momager and replaced her with her sister. We hope that works out better for her, but can't help noting that it couldn't have been very fun firing your own mom.

Paula Dorn, co-founder of the BizParentz Foundation, a nonprofit corporation providing education, advocacy, and charitable support to parents and children engaged in the entertainment industry, paints a grimmer picture. "It seems as though many inexperienced parents believe they should be taking on career-enhancing tasks for their child without understanding what is appropriate."

Familial and friendship support should always be used with discretion.

Still, it's understandable that people gravitate toward working with those they can relate to, those who have "automatic" skin in the game, because you *will* be close to your manager if the relationship's any good. Even if you can keep your family and friends out of your business, it is our belief that, in today's career-heavy world, the talent-management or manager-client relationship is one of the most important in a person's life, and it can stand alongside relationships with parents, children, siblings, spouses, and truly close friends to vie for your daily focus and attention. Like those other relationships, the manager-talent connection requires trust, demands patience, and induces growth. Coasting simply won't do.

Not all "local" or "automatic" managers are created equal. Michael has created this hair-raising chart (see next page),[2] which indicates the basic tenets of Objectivity versus Skin in the Game as demonstrated in relationships with Rabbi/Priest/Imam, Therapist, Coach, Boss, Agent/Manager, Family Member, Spouse, and Best Friend.

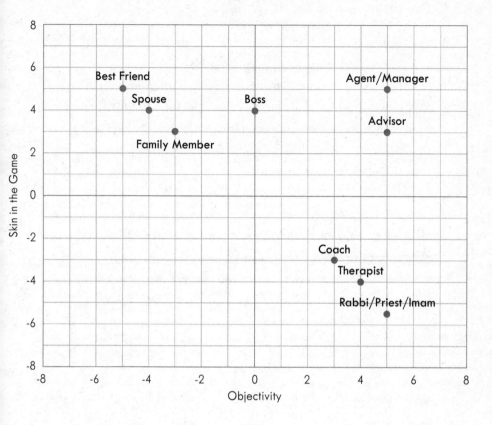

Obviously, the positions are "ballpark" but the takeaways embedded here are not to be ignored:

- A boss—a good boss, that is—will likely have the greatest balance of skin in the game and objectivity, but they don't have an excess of either. They want what's best for you, and your destiny affects them, but not the way it affects your family. (In Chapter 8, we'll talk about how you can cultivate skin in the game from those who manage you.)
- Your best bud, your uncle, and your spouse have a lot more skin in the game than they do objectivity. What happens to you will likely affect them fairly directly; so much so, in fact, that they

probably can't do the proper distancing necessary for the strongest advice.

- Your coach, therapist, or religious guide bring greater objectivity, but at the end of the day, their investment is not as life-or-death as family members and spouses.
- Only the agent/manager can provide high levels of skin in the game matched by full-force objectivity. It's their raison d'être, the nature of their occupation.

Sometimes you may need to mix and match to get all the best elements for strong management from more than one source. Once skin in the game is firmly in place, strong management can deliver an invaluable dimension to the talent it represents, what we call the Third Party Effect. We'll go there next.

SKIN IN THE GAME FOR MANAGERS

0x Management	Doesn't have any focus or understanding why alignment is important. Charges should do what they are asked because it is their job.
5x Management	Knows that having skin in the game with the team is a very important element of trust, but is not clear how to create it and communicate it.
10x Management	Helps to create a cohesive team and can articulate how everyone's success is tied to one another, knowing and demonstrating that their recommendations are beneficial to each team member, because their destinies are connected.

SKIN IN THE GAME FOR TALENT

0x Talent	Doesn't really understand that giving people a vested interest in their life/career has concrete value. Believes people should help out of the goodness of their hearts.
5x Talent	Knows that having partners with skin in the game can be a huge boon to their goals, but has yet to identify who can play that role, and doesn't know how to secure the right person.
10x Talent	Creates a team filled with alignment where wins are shared with those around them and vice versa.

TAKEAWAYS FROM CHAPTER 6

- Skin in the game is our catchall phrase for the high level of investment every strong manager needs in their talent, and talent needs in their manager.
- Strong managers are after much more than a percentage. They have an emotional and spiritual stake in the talent's future. They believe.
- Really and truly loving what a talent does is the healthiest starting place for management. Deep respect and trust are the best starting place for the talent.
- Skin in the game is the most honest, most logical way to build trust with a prospective talent. Once the talent knows your wagons are hitched, trust follows.
- Smart talent will listen to a manager's sometimes difficult advice, as long as the talent knows that manager has skin in the game.
- It takes a visionary, empathetic sensibility to lead great talent.
- Ultimately, the management-talent connection is symbiotic: the two entities succeed or fail together.

1 2 3 4 5 6 **7** 8 9 10

THE THIRD PARTY EFFECT

He who represents himself has a fool for a client.
—ABRAHAM LINCOLN

I n the 1979 French film *L'associé* (The Associate), a down-on-his-luck investor creates a make-believe business partner in a last-ditch attempt to save the biz. What happens next is as telling as it is hilarious: Playing the imaginary associate, the man finds "his voice," business booms like crazy, new clients sign on in droves, and the man's wife even announces that she's fallen in love with the partner—all despite the fact that he doesn't exist.

As silly as it sounds, the movie is a perfect illustration of what we call the Third Party Effect.

Imagine telling someone that you're amazing at what you do. Now imagine someone else, someone credible, saying the same thing about you. The message is always stronger coming from a third party. When you say, "I went to Harvard, worked in senior management at Facebook, and created the open-source language that runs half the internet," you sound like a conceited jerk.

If someone else says those very same words about you, you sound like a unicorn.

In a court of law, it's never advisable to represent yourself, and the same goes for talent. The tendency will always be to oversell or undersell, and either way, there is virtually no credibility where there is no objectivity. The Third Party Effect removes your ego, high and low, and shows the listener that someone else out there believes in you enough to put their own reputation on the line.

One other thing to keep in mind: Most people don't have great management and struggle to get it. While most companies in the industry are desperate to find and work with great tech talent, as of this writing, our own company has a five-thousand-person-plus waiting list of tech talent hoping to engage our management services. This is because the talent knows if they work with us, they get people with skin in their game who can give them the benefit of the Third Party Effect. The recommendation of a third party (and especially one who has skin in the game) automatically implies value and is one of the few ways to rise above the din.

THE UNDERSELLERS

Long before we took on the management of supercoders, we understood that, on the whole, they had a tendency to sell themselves short. Back in the days when we were mostly music biz managers, we often had to hire tech talent to build out our artists' websites, as well as apps for the entertainment world, so we already had a fair amount of experience working with skilled (and sometimes not-so-skilled) programmers. What we observed on a consistent basis was that the tech talent did not know their own worth. They would come to the negotiation table with financial figures that were not only lower than what we expected them to ask for, but were lower than what the market would claim they were worth.

It was a real head scratcher.

Without a definite plan in mind, we got to work and did some research in order to determine the real market value of these mavens. As soon as we started 10x Management, we instantly raised the asking price for our tech talent, first, because we armed ourselves with better data about what they could command, and second, because we had the luxury of being an out-side party, two guys who were so impressed by their considerable talents that we could sing their praises in ways that they never could.

An outside party can afford to not be wounded by criticism, rejection, blowback, or indifference.

A realistic outside party can state an asking price without the slightest bit of doubt, shame, or fear.

A realistic, credible outside party can hype without sounding ridiculous and bring context without sounding far-fetched.

To this day, we'll sit in on pitch meetings with partners and hear them try to sell themselves. Even when they mean well, they usually sound like inept boasters. Often, that's where we'll step in and ask if they wouldn't like to have us, or some other outside entity, singing their praises.

We've also experienced the opposite of boasting, an aversion to exposing and expressing one's true worth—especially among tech talent. Unfortunately, the self-effacing wallflower technique doesn't work either.

Our former co-founder was himself a savvy technologist who also happened to be uncomfortable with representing himself. When we first met and began repping him as his agent for his software engineering, he never wanted to tell people that he had gone to Harvard or speak of his many other outstanding accomplishments. He knew how bad it would sound from his mouth and was just too uncomfortable to ask for market rate or explain why he was worth it. The result was that he regularly got paid about a third below his basic market value. Ironically, as soon as he started repping other technologists, he crushed it. He could sell anyone—anyone but himself, that is.

Just like the French movie we mentioned at the top of this chapter, we had a client named Rafik who, before meeting us, would sometimes call up employers disguised as another person and act as an agent for himself. It's not entirely ethical, but the ploy worked so well that some of Rafik's coder friends signed him on to be their fake agent, too. It seems that anyone else negotiating on your behalf will usually get better results, even if they have little experience or reputation.

The Third Party Effect isn't just about managers and agents speaking for their talent. In the corporate world, whenever bosses go to the powers that be and fight to get their star employee better compensation, you are seeing the Third Party Effect in action. When our client Sean took a job at a major international bank, he made sure his hires had our outside compensation representation. By doing this, he was, in essence, guaranteeing them the Third Party Effect (with an entity that had skin in the game), to bolster his hiring decisions and ensure that the people he was bringing in got the best deal possible. Before they even walked in the door, he showed them he had their backs and would engender trust before they began. He knew that this might cost the institution more money per employee, but it would ensure getting the exact team he needed, which would, in turn, make the bank that much more successful. The Third Party Effect is everywhere someone, with skin in the game, acts as your advocate.

The Third Party Effect isn't just about advocacy though; it's also about defense. For instance, if ever a client or customer is aggressive with someone on our staff, we always step in to protect our people, full force. This breeds loyalty from our team members and keeps them feeling safe, knowing that someone has their back. It also allows them to take risks.

We're sorry to report that many in the corporate world still believe they're better off deploying a duck-and-cover policy when one of their people is in the hot seat. This strategy might have been a normative part of work culture long ago. Today, it's an invitation for your team to look elsewhere. The new workforce—10xers and non-10xers, millennials and non-millennials—want and expect their bosses to stand up and protect them, and why shouldn't they? It's the classy thing to do and, besides, it pays dividends in all directions. In the Hollywood movie version, it's the hero who stands in harm's way to protect others. Any time people fight for you because they know you're great, they demonstrate their ability to be a positive third party on your behalf, and you love them for it.

Those are the leaders we will follow anywhere.

Combined, skin in the game and the Third Party Effect are a one-two, knock-out punch. With these elements at the ready, strong management is equipped to represent the full breadth and scope of whatever talent is after—their true goals, true drives, true needs. This combo is also the best weapon in dealmaking, when it's time to employ a flexible negotiation strategy and win big. (We'll talk more about that in Chapter 10.)

There's one more benefit to the Third Party Effect that's so obvious it's practically invisible. Any time a manager is speaking on your behalf, they are ipso facto presenting a "second opinion," since you obviously also believe in yourself (we hope!) Thus, when the Third Party speaks, it's as if you and your manager really make up two voices in agreement, and two voices make a chorus.

BISHOP'S CHECKMATE

For world-class supercoder Bryan Bishop, the implementation of a third party was crucial to his development, but it wasn't the obvious move at first. He started as a true solo renegade. Bishop grew up in Austin, Texas, and was already a programming ace by middle school.

"I was into video games, and in particular, video game hacking and reverse engineering," he explains. "I was very adept at using something called the *GameShark*, which was a device that sat between a game cartridge and a game console, and it allowed you to manipulate the game's memory."

After he broke the fourth wall in video games, he branched out into the thicket of the internet and quickly developed an acumen for complex web development. Fueled by super-brain-power and unstoppable digital ambition, it was a natural progression, but he was mostly self-taught and self-directed.

When we took him on, Bishop's accomplishments were many, even though he was barely twenty, but over time our partnership transformed him into a highly sought-after blockchain/bitcoin expert, commanding anywhere between $600 and $1,000 an hour. Interestingly, he himself doesn't see the relationship as talent-management. Like Barbara Carr in our previous chapter, Bishop experiences the relationship between parties as symbiotic.

"I've never quite agreed with the word *manager*. It may be true that Michael and Rishon are technically my managers in public, but I call them my *talent*, because that's how I think of them. Even in the bitcoin community where my arrangement is pretty unique, the sense I get is that people don't really understand just how aligned 10x Management and I really are. People ask, 'Are they recruiters?' No. There's nothing recruiter-like about our relationship whatsoever. They are long-term business partners that I have chosen to work with, who provide tremendous value to me."

For Bishop, the choice of bringing in a third party wasn't obvious at first. "I'm not completely incompetent at sales. I can do sales. But frankly speaking, my primary skill is programming. And in programming, it's very common to talk about *context-switching*. Well, switching to sales drains programmers, it impacts your productivity. And it was draining me."

(This is a strong example of disrupting the "flow state" we describe in Chapter 1.)

Even by supercoder standards, Bishop is a true adventurer. Talking to him, one sometimes feels as if they've dialed into the future via a time machine. In addition to his blockchain/bitcoin work, Bishop has a serious interest in biotech and its implications on DNA, including a commercial venture involving human genetic engineering, also known as genetic modification, using human embryos, and reprogramming sperm stem cells to generate genetically modified sperm. He also holds patents pending on using DNA as a massive digital storage device (like a hard drive).

Toto, we aren't playing video games in Kansas anymore.

"I recently got involved in a company called Genomic Prediction," Bishop says, "and they do embryo screening, or genetic testing of embryos. It was such an interesting opportunity and they had a need for my skills and expertise in software development."

MIT Technology Review recently described the New Jersey-based start-up as purveyors of "a hotly debated new genetic test being called '23andMe, but on embryos.'"[1] Bishop concedes that some of what he does raises serious ethical questions. To our great satisfaction, he has turned to us to hash out these issues.

"10x has been very generous with their time, reviewing the implications of some of these topics with me," he says. "Even if they don't completely agree with me, they're a dedicated sounding board, and they know how to communicate my ideas to others. Biology is a form of technology. Genetics is a form of programming. The ability to program biology is going to unlock all sorts of possibilities and opportunities. In fact, I believe that in the future, we're going to look back and say that what we did before genetic engineering was barbaric and like playing a genetic lottery on our children."

Bishop knows that his take is not necessarily the popular one, especially since one of the practitioners of this work was recently sentenced to three years in a Chinese prison. "Right now, there's a very intense culture of conservative values and a push to not rock the boat or try new things. There's an immense social pressure on people in academia, too, to not do certain things yet. But I'm not a member of academia. I'm an independent individual with my own means and my own plans and ideas. And I don't necessarily agree that it's better to let someone suffer from an illness because the drug that treats their condition has not yet been approved by regulators. Still, I understand that there are many people who disagree with me, and 10x Management helps me navigate those waters."

Above and beyond these ethical debates, Bishop's relationship to managerial guidance transcends income requirements and lifestyle choices, email editing, or gig interviews. He is a living embodiment of the right way to deploy third party representation.

"The guys at 10x are acutely aware of how I present myself out there in the world. I'm very technical and detail-oriented, and to people who focus on technical details, we assume that other people are really focused on them, too, right? But sometimes, when closing a deal, the details are not what people are actually judging. They might be looking at track record, experience, reputation, brand, or even how polite you are, how responsive you are, things like that. One of their roles is to engage them at their level, to bring in things that I would have forgotten or not have realized to even mention.

"In the clinch, I can even forget about some of my prior experience, just totally forget to bring it up, you know? I was recently talking with someone who wants me to develop a big security solution for storing bitcoin claims, and I forgot to mention that, hey, I've developed a system that is currently storing over $50 million. Maybe I should have mentioned that!?"

The benefits of third party representation for a game changer at Bishop's level are obvious and instantaneous. It means that he can focus on doing great work. In ultra-high-tech, this need for representation grows exponentially. As author William Gibson purportedly puts it, "The future is already here, it's just not evenly distributed." Advanced tech is forever in a state of research and preimplementation, with an emphasis on speed. This creates a challenge for the third party rep, who bridges the gap between civilian understanding and arcane elite knowledge.

"A lot of people would be very surprised to learn just what sort of technologies are actually possible today. Let me tell you, my mom has no idea what I do for a living. If I tried to explain what a compiler is to her, her brains would start melting! Because, if you think about it, some forms of computation basically look like magic. Any sufficiently advanced technology is indistinguishable from magic. As my reps, Michael and Rishon can help the other side understand what's possible."

One thing I've learned is that I'm not the owner
of my talent; I'm the manager of it.
—MADONNA, 2004

THIRD PARTYING

Even though we have represented talent for more than twenty-five years, we still sought out someone with skin in the game and a Third Party Effect to represent us when it came time to sell this book. We consider ourselves negotiation experts and are comfortable diving into new industries and new kinds of deals with somewhat reckless abandon. But it's important to note that those capabilities still don't make it smart for us to represent ourselves. Much like our clients, we hate representing ourselves in any transaction.

We know, for all the reasons laid out in this chapter, that someone else, someone credible, will likely do a better job. That's why we sought out literary representation from someone we could trust. Agents need agents and managers need managers. Knowledge and capability are no substitute for the Third Party Effect.

Lucky for us, the literary agent we found, Lucinda Halpern, deeply understands both the vital power and the immeasurable nuances of third party testimony. The very fact that you're reading this book is living proof that she knows what she's doing.

Like ourselves, Lucinda got her start managing music artists from Brooklyn. Unlike us, Lucinda was first a child opera singer with real-time stage experience, so she knew firsthand what it felt like to be the artist. Managing bands, she had no credentials per se—she just picked up the phone and started hustling. When she realized she could transfer these skills to the book world where her true passions were, she started knocking on doors, literary agency to literary agency, pitching herself as a marketing manager. "I quickly learned that if you can't get in the front door, try the side door."

To prove her mettle, Lucinda was given the charge to go out there and sell books, and that's just what she did. "It was about as scrappy as it gets. I had to use my network to find good candidates, good authors to take on. I dug into the agency's slush pile and when I found someone I believed in, I'd shoot up my hands and say, 'Let me work with this author!'" She took some dangerous gambles, closed a string of big deals, and discovered she had a real knack for representation.

"Talent has to live and breathe what they're doing, day in and day out," Lucinda explains. "It takes a different kind of energy. When you're the third party, the pressure is off in a way, and you can take the longer view."

Heading her own agency, Lucinda has amassed a stable of unique authors. She won't play third party for just anybody though.

"For me to represent someone, I not only need to love that person's work. I also need to know that the person I'm representing is going to be every bit as hardworking as I am and willing to do whatever it takes to keep up momentum. In other words, I need to know that this person is a visionary—as in, someone with a personal vision that they're going to stick with."

Lucinda echoes Barbara Carr here—vision is the shared territory for talent and management.

Agents are often likened to therapists, and being a third party representative—whether it's a literary agent, a music manager, or a corporate team leader—can be an exercise in psychology. "You need to know what kind of person you're dealing with," Lucinda says. "You need to know the level of feedback and the tone of feedback that will work, how it will land. Because your goal is to keep the talent on track. You have to edit yourself down in the interest of keeping people motivated, enthusiastic, and positive."

The manager, playing third party, is the living embodiment of enthusiasm for what a particular talent is doing, or is capable of doing. They're often the first person that gives credibility to a talent's idea, and they become a champion for that idea as an expert themselves in a particular industry. This aspect of the role is key for effective third party testimony.

"From the book editor's point of view," Lucinda explains, "when a good agent says, 'This manuscript is something I think can sell,' there's this stab of recognition and validation. And if the editor trusts you, they'll listen."

Lucinda points out that third partying sometimes involves speaking out of both sides of your mouth, a challenge for those who strive for integrity. "You're telling your talent one thing—to keep them motivated and excited. But on the other hand, you're dealing with editors who are often giving you every reason why a book won't work. It's tough because you have to keep your own enthusiasm high in the face of skepticism."

This "double agent" quality cuts to the prismatic complexity of the third party POV. The strong manager or representative needs to foster credibility on both sides, grounded in realities. Yes, you rep the talent, and you're playing third party for them, first and foremost. But to be a really good third party advocate, you have to know and, to some degree, respect the needs of the other side of the table. The recipients of your message need to believe you are an honest representative, allergic to hyperbole, and only enthusiastic when the level of talent genuinely warrants it.

This ability to see and discourse with both sides, bridging gaps and coming to terms, is the highest level of third party representation.

"In book publishing," Lucinda explains, "these editors are inundated with pitches and false information around the clock. How can you break out of that? First, from having a personality that people want to deal with. Second, they need to come to trust your taste. And then, of course, they need to be convinced by the pitch at hand. If they know who you are and how you work, that background informs their instinctive reception of your pitch."

Sometimes referred to as the middleman or gatekeeper, the manager/agent/third party rep is there to protect the recipient from red herrings.

"These are long-term relationships I'm building, and I want to be known to be authentic when I act as a third party advocate," Lucinda says. "I'm not going to take on a high volume of projects and send things to editors that I don't really believe in, because they can feel it. When my enthusiasm is genuine, they can feel it."

THE HONING DEVICE

In December of 2011, our old friend and renowned entertainment business manager, Phil Sarna, invited us to his legendary holiday party. Over the years, Phil's gained a reputation for throwing these fetes in interesting locations. This time the shindig took place in a garage that was about to be torn down to make way for yet another high-end condo. At the party, Phil mentioned to us that his longtime client, the multiplatinum-selling, Grammy-nominated musician Vanessa Carlton was starting to talk to new managers.

What Phil didn't yet know is that we'd been following Vanessa's career closely for many years already. Rishon and his wife actually went on a double-date in early 2002 with Vanessa and a former client of ours whom she was sorta kinda seeing at the time. She also ran a marathon to benefit Musicians On Call. More important, we had a copy of her 2011 CD *Rabbits on the Run* in the office, and we played it constantly, knocked out by both the artistry of the album and how markedly different it was from her earlier works, yet still distinctly Vanessa.

This was an artist capable of growth.

At Phil's behest, we visited her in her Soho loft. First impressions count. Vanessa was utterly down to earth, smart, grounded. She'd experienced so much in her career already, and she knew very clearly what she did and didn't want. This jumped out for us. Knowing what you don't want is as important as knowing what you do want, and it's the mark of a true 10xer.

Vanessa wanted to be an artist.

She didn't want to be a product, manufactured and disposable.

She knew how to work hard, and she had realistic expectations to match her musical sophistication. This is a person who moved to New York on her own at age fourteen to attend the School of American Ballet, signed her first record deal as a teenager, and had a multiplatinum album and Grammy nominations in the first minutes of her twenties.

She played us some demos that day, the songs that ultimately turned into the masterful *Liberman*, still one of the greatest albums we've ever worked on.

In one meeting, we were sold. This time, our instincts were on the money.

As we entered our eighth year working together, we completed a ten-week run of Vanessa playing the lead role in the Broadway production of *Beautiful: The Carole King Musical*—playing Carole King, that is—and we're on the precipice of completing Vanessa's next album, *Love Is An Art*, being released into the world as we write this book. From where we stand, it feels like we're just getting started with Vanessa, and we can't wait to see what the next eight years have in store.

It's also a personal triumph for us, because the relationship we've enjoyed with her is one of the most productive and rewarding partnerships we've experienced in twenty-five years in the biz. That's not to take anything away from the other artists on our roster, but it's very rare in one's career to connect with an artist on as many levels. At least in part, it's a testament to Vanessa's maturity and to her 10x-level manageability.

For someone with a voice as beautiful as Vanessa's, off-the-chart piano chops, and songwriting to match, it's also a mark of her character that she knows when to let the third party do the talking for her.

"I simply cannot sell myself," she explains. "I'm not that great at networking, and I don't even really know how to talk about myself in that manner. I'm too close to the subject matter. In fact, the only way I know how to represent what I do is to make records and play music."

When a talent is as laser-focused on their art as Vanessa is, finding the right representation can sometimes be like having a great weight lifted. Just as with supercoder Bryan Bishop, Vanessa has been set free to do her work, simply by trusting that strategic communication is taking place on her behalf.

Still, the fact is, she's been through a few managers over the years, and it hasn't always worked. She insists that it's important to have the *right* third party doing the talking.

"I've noticed that when I wasn't working with the right manager, I would often end up in situations that I didn't feel comfortable in. I would start to second guess my music, and the worst part was, I would fear taking artistic risks. With a great third party rep, you really feel like you can soar." When you have the protection of great management, you get to take risks, make bold choices, learn new things, and fail as needed. Without the freedom to do that, talent of all kinds often end up feeling stuck and vulnerable in a bad way.

In true 10x fashion, Vanessa goes out of her way to learn how to help us help her. She's a blackbelt at showing up, and there's always an element of gratitude in our dealings with her. Real 10x talents understand that gratitude fuels productivity. "When you feel represented," she explains, "everything changes. The freedom to do more and grow more just goes way up."

One thing Vanessa told us has been echoed again and again with interviewees from every conceivable field: Whoever represents you, whoever plays Third Party for you, they *must* feel passionate about your work.

"But," Vanessa adds, "they've also got to be a clear communicator."

This clarity is no small thing, for at bottom, the Third Party Effect is an act of translation. In fact, one of the key "side bonuses" of the Third Party Effect is the way it helps hone the shape of just what a talent is selling. Better than any CV, a good Third Party spiel gives space for the recipient to experience the talent. This, in turn, frequently helps an artist discover the right "frame" for what they're doing.

"Over time, I've become a better communicator myself as a direct result of working with good management. These guys . . . they show me what good interpersonal communication in our industry is all about."

OFFICE PARTY

As with skin in the game, we want to make absolutely clear that the benefits of the Third Party Effect do not only play out in formalized manager-talent relations. The Third Party Effect is *in* effect whenever someone credible speaks on your behalf—and whether you are an employee in a giant corporation or a roaming freelancer on the cusp of your next engagement, you would be wise to ask yourself: Who can be *my* Third Party? Who can deliver my message with the most credibility, the most clarity, and the greatest impact?

On the other side, if you're the manager or team leader, you should also be asking who you most need to advocate for, and who most deserves your praise or your sales pitch, because being a Third Party is a core component of your role whether you know it or not.

The late CEO Mark Hurd, a legendary tech executive who served as co-CEO and board member of Oracle Corporation, saw Third Party praise as one of the great lost arts in leadership. As he put it on an episode of *Business Insider*'s "This is Success" podcast,[2] there was a time long ago when "it was just an unspoken value in the company that if you could sit around and brag about all the great people you developed in the company who are now in senior positions, this was a merit badge. This was something you wore on your sleeve." Hurd lamented that this irreplaceable value has faded with time in corporate culture, due to "mercenary hiring" and a deterioration of mentorship practices.

According to Hurd, "You would come out of college, and you would go to work at a company, and you would actually get trained by the company. You'd have trainers, enablers, people that would help you, teach you about how to sell, how to listen, how to communicate…. Training was looked at as an investment, not as an expense."

To counter the trend, Hurd developed a "Class of" program that paired new college grads with a manager-mentor. "There was no stock option for it," Hurd said. "It was just a source of pride."

Hurd was on to something in ways he couldn't have predicted. Today, shorter job tenures, hiring for specialized skill sets, and on-the-fly training have created an overriding need for more substantial mentorship and advocacy in the workplace. The need itself may well be creating a natural turn in the tides.

In another recent piece on Inc.com, writer Firas Kittaneh explores "3 Ways Leaders Can Become Outstanding Advocates for Their Team.[3] Kittaneh cites an MSW Research and Dale Carnegie Training study that contends that the relationship with one's immediate supervisor is one of the key drivers of "employee engagement," that must-have harbinger of loyalty and growth.

Team leaders, the article contends, must do the following to stay relevant:

- Listen to employee concerns and carry them up the organizational chart.
- Share performance results and positive feedback with other departments.
- Seek out growth opportunities for young performers.

These three directives are like a beautiful primer in New School management. Know that 10xers expect nothing less.

In our next chapter, we'll turn the Old School workplace pyramid on its head and delve into the new multidirectional art of conducting business, a little something we call 360° Management.

THE THIRD PARTY EFFECT FOR MANAGERS

0x Management	Does not understand the value of having others sing their praises and often spends a lot of time tooting their own horn, sounding like an ass, and stealing credit for the work of others.
5x Management	Sees the value of having someone else sing their praises, and even sometimes does this for people on their team, but has yet to figure out how to get their own praises sung at the right time by others.
10x Management	Not only goes to bat for their team at every turn, which builds the value of the team and thereby increases their own value, but also gets very strategic with who and how to ask during those times that they need an advocate.

THE THIRD PARTY EFFECT FOR TALENT

0x Talent	Does not understand the value of having others sing their praises, or doing the same for others, and spends a lot of time tooting their own horn, making most people around them want to barf.
5x Talent	Knows they can't run around saying how great they are, and, therefore, is seeking other ways to get the positive halo put over them. Has started to do this for others, calling out people's great work in the hopes that it will be returned.
10x Talent	Really understands the value of having Third Party advocates, and is creating them, by requesting that other people introduce them or their ideas, knowing that the natural byproduct will be better than any other method of self-expression. Seeks people in their lives who can do this actively and strategically for them, whether it be a manager, lawyer, coach, friend, or team member.

TAKEAWAYS FROM CHAPTER 7

- The Third Party Effect happens every time somebody advocates on your behalf.
- Having a credible Third Party speak on your behalf is the only real (and certainly the best) way to get people to understand your value and your mission.
- Self-promoters will always tend to oversell or undersell themselves. They may succeed in spite of this but at a hefty cost to credibility.
- A realistic, credible Third Party can negotiate on your behalf without being guided by fear, shame, or doubt.
- Third Partying means acting as a credible, reliable translator of values and ideas, a kind of "double agent" that fosters respect and understanding on both sides.
- A good Third Party can also help the talent learn how to better frame or discuss themselves, by honing in on just what it is that talent is offering.
- Readers who exhibit a willingness to act as Third Party advocates will engender the most loyalty and best performance from their people.

1 2 3 4 5 6 7 **8** 9 10

360° MANAGEMENT

> It doesn't make sense to hire smart people and tell them what
> to do. We hire smart people so they can tell us what to do.
> —STEVE JOBS

THE BIRD'S EYE VIEW

In the previous chapter, we began to explore what we identified as the *symbiotic* relationship between talent and management. Merriam-Webster defines "symbiotic" as "characterized by, or being, a close, cooperative, or interdependent relationship."

Now we turn our attention to the symbiotic relationship between employees and managers. "Close, cooperative, and interdependent" is the optimal state of affairs.

In the hierarchy of the workplace, most of us have people below us, people above us, and people adjacent to us. We also have myriad people who are in other departments, people who are neither our bosses nor our direct reports.

In order for a company to have the greatest chance for a 10x-level culture, the management of talent has to flow in all directions. It is among the highest priorities for those with power to create an environment where this can exist.

To state it another way, no team can function at its best in an atmosphere where a subordinate does not feel comfortable sharing ideas with people above and adjacent to them.

Moreover, as each talent rises through the ranks, they will likely manage more people. This means that the spirit in which they were "raised" by the company will proliferate, for better or worse.

To foster a culture of support, openness, and safety, those *above* you need to protect you and give you the latitude to express your ideas in full; those *adjacent* to you need to feel sufficiently empowered to help sing your praises and receive praise from you; and those *beneath* you must be emboldened to offer you support and come to you with their ideas, challenges, and disasters. Good will and empowerment rarely "trickle down" and they certainly are even less likely to "trickle up." The spirit of close, cooperative interdependence has to emanate everywhere, and flow freely between all involved parties.

Without a culture of symbiotic positivity, you can guess what happens. Political infighting festers, the aggressive push aside the meek, and an environment of cagey silence pervades, top to bottom. To anyone who has experienced this kind of workplace—and, unfortunately, most have at least once in their career—it would not be an overstatement to call it a living nightmare of toxicity. In today's economy it's worse than a nightmare, because that kind of environment is going to turn off the best and brightest, and once you lose the talent war, you completely limit a company's ability to compete and excel.

If the spirit of symbiotic positivity seems like a universally acknowledged good, it's also true that, historically, the opposite spirit often prevails. To this day, many company management cultures err on the side of fear, silence, and "every person for themselves."

Moreover, even when relations are not adversarial, there can exist a natural disconnect between those who run the day-to-day and those who build the future. Ralph Perrine, director of the award-winning Innovation Garage, which powers a portfolio of solutions for the healthcare industry understands this need to build bridges in all directions.

"When our team starts to design or code something new, we have that natural innovator's excitement," Perrine explains, "But it's unfair to expect everyone else to automatically feel that excitement right off the bat."

"Our customer ecosystem is made up of stakeholders—auditors, security and privacy teams, infrastructure support, customer support—who will all play a role in the eventual impact and customer experience of the solution we are building. These stakeholders have a right not to be excited—at least until they understand how the new solution works and how it impacts their goals and areas of responsibility."

"This actually works in our favor. We have gained a lot by listening and learning from those who are not automatically excited about new things."

In a hilarious analogy, Perrine likens this disjointed state of affairs to the plight of the inventor of the pooper scooper. "The guy who invented it was probably thrilled about it. But for the rest of us, it's just a tool we have to use in the morning when we take the dog out. So there's sort of this gap between the excitement that the innovator feels versus the attitude of the people who end up owning and operating that innovation later on."

For Perrine, 10x development means not only finding a way to communicate your passion, but also finding a way to absorb the other party's skepticism. "Driving change is hard," he says. "Over time, I've learned that our products improve when we're willing to hear others tell us the many ways things might go wrong."

360° Management—not to be confused with 360° reviews—is our prescriptive measure for building bridges and thriving in the workplace. It's about turning your managers, your peers, and your underlings into the great managers we've described in this book. We understand that 360° Management is an aspirational ideal, but the striving itself is a crucial step on the road to an individual and/or a company becoming 10x.

Dealing with your manager is often the hardest part of any job. Not every manager has the tools, the training, or the proclivity to be great at guiding others. It's a truism that people often rise to their level of incompetence and nowhere is this more evident than with regard to managerial style. The top brass are not always those with the highest EQ. After all, the difference between management and leadership is huge.

There's also "your place in things" to consider. In most environments, you can't go to your boss's boss and ask them to get your boss to be a better manager—at least not on a regular basis.

Therefore, in order to get the guidance and representation you need, it will be necessary to manage your manager and your peers, with the same dedication that you hopefully manage your charges (if you have them).

Sometimes, ironically enough, dealing with underlings can be a manager's worst angle. Dr. Audrey Weiner, former CEO of The New Jewish Home, told us about a large healthcare organization who engaged an external firm to conduct a series of extensive evaluations of senior and middle managers. It was an elaborate process, including direct feedback to each manager along with consultation with the CEO, followed by coaching sessions to address relevant issues. When the C Suite manager participated in this process, the results were particularly informative, and not altogether positive.

"He was skilled in managing up, and in working with his peers," Weiner says. "However, those who reported to him spoke of his lack of supervision, training, and responsiveness to issues. Even with coaching he was never able to make the needed changes to be successful in his role."

As Weiner notes, uncovering the problem is never enough. Each individual has to be willing and able to "look 360°," acknowledge room for improvement in every direction, *and* be willing to invest the energy and time it takes to accomplish real change—a series of growth spurts that, she maintains, will only take place about half the time.

"At this particular organization," she adds, "when this individual couldn't change, several team members chose to move on to other organizations."

That's the price you pay for not taking the need for 360° Management seriously.

For today's dedicated worker, everywhere on the chain, there's a bonus aspect to 360° Management that's also worth mentioning: By taking an active role in the flow of managerial guidance both to and from you in every direction, you are taking responsibility for your own destiny and fully embracing the understanding of interdependence that exists in organizations. That's what being 10x is all about.

> Train people well enough so they can leave,
> treat them well enough so they don't want to.
> —RICHARD BRANSON

HOW MUCH MANAGEMENT
IS MANAGEMENT ENOUGH?

In a two-year study on team performance recently covered by Laura Delizonna, PhD, in *Harvard Business Review*,[1] Google revealed that the highest-performing teams have one thing in common: psychological safety, or the belief that you won't be punished if you make a mistake. As Paul Santagata, Head of Industry at Google put it, "Our success hinges on the ability to take risks and be vulnerable in front of peers." This data is particularly valuable because, well, if there is anything Google does well, it's data.

Santagata posits six steps to bolster a safe atmosphere: 1) Approach conflict as a collaborator, not an adversary; 2) Speak human to human; 3) Anticipate reactions and plan countermoves; 4) Replace blame with curiosity; 5) Ask for feedback on delivery; and 6) Measure for safety.

Step Number 6 is germane to our vision of 360° Management. For our money, great management and the sense of safety it can engender is a corporation's greatest invisible asset.

However, a sense of safety is not what people usually think of when they think of management.

Betterworks recently ran a piece called "People Hate Being Managed—What Organizations (And Managers) Need to Do Instead,"[2] in which author Deborah Holstein points out that only 1 in 7 employees believe performance reviews inspire them to improve. "Newsflash," she writes, "No one WANTS to be managed. Even the term 'manage' evokes feelings of control and manipulation."

Holstein astutely recognizes that the roadblock to good management is usually found in a lack of bespoke practices. "If an employee receives feedback from their manager who's been only loosely involved in their development," she explains, "they're far more likely to reject any constructive criticism they receive. It's only natural. If they don't feel that their manager truly knows them, their work, and their strengths, why would they believe that their manager has a good grasp on where they need to improve? Many employees who find themselves in this situation will question whether their manager is even qualified to be giving them feedback. And when the review process is closely tied to earning a bonus, raise, or promotion, employees can't afford to be open to feedback, both figuratively and literally."

Great bespoke management is hard to find, but what would the workplace look like with no management at all? In a curious and telling counter-example on the importance of good management, Amazon-owned Zappos' CEO Tony Hsieh recently tried to abolish traditional managerial roles by implementing a system called *Holacracy*.[3] According to *Business Insider*, this self-management program is the creation of Brian Robertson, a former software developer and entrepreneur turned management guru. Through Holacracy, Hsieh and Robertson advocate a workflow that allows engineers to develop ideas utterly without the direction of a manager.

On the surface, it sounds great. Work is processed through "roles" that are always subject to change. For instance, an employee who isn't a marketer can take on the marketing role, in addition to whatever other roles they hold down, should they get the urge. In lieu of management, Holacracy implements what Robertson calls "lead links"—people who assign roles and represent "their circle," but with one key difference: These "links" are in no way responsible for the individuals they oversee.

It is not a surprise to us that Hsieh's noble experiment has had some serious casualties. When Hsieh's email call for Holacracy hit the company server, the organization divided three ways, between believers, nonbelievers, and those who "decided to remain out of convenience, despite their reservations." All official titles were abolished, and 14 percent of the company—a whopping 210 employees—voluntarily hit the road.

As one disgruntled employee put it, with the move toward Holacracy, "Employees are in constant fear of losing their jobs for saying or doing something that proves to management that they aren't a 'culture fit.'" Another employee described the change as a gear-shift toward a "disruptive atmosphere" that included "bothersome social experiments." One beleaguered employee gave the company a two-star rating and bemoaned the fact that top brass would allow so many strong employees to leave just to bolster an ideology.

To us, this story has a plain and simple lesson: *No management* is definitely not the answer. *Less management* is frequently not the answer either. What the modern company needs is a game changing program of 360° Management for everyone—flexible, agile, human-centered, and fear-free.

One of the most important after-effects of 360° Management is that it often weeds out those who aren't a good cultural fit for a given organization. There have been several instances in our own careers where we had the wrong people on various projects. Sometimes these people were employees, sometimes they were clients, and in a few unfortunate cases they were even business partners. In each of these instances, we waited far too long to take action. In fact, truth be told, we usually took no action at all. In many of these cases, we waited until someone else took action. Not only did we want to give someone endless "benefit of the doubt," we really believed in our heart of hearts that, if we made the correct moves, we could get these individuals to "straighten up and fly right" (and by *right*, we mean the way we wanted).

Was our excessive tolerance due to an unconscious desire to be given the same latitude should we fail ourselves? Or did we merely have an aversion to the conflict we thought might ensue should we address matters directly? The answer is anyone's guess, but the long and short of it is we clung to several bad work relationships way past their sell-by date. This has been a really hard pattern for us to live through. We pride ourselves on the ability to evolve and improve quickly when presented with good information, but with this challenge we seemed to repeat mistakes over and over and, what's more, we had to live with the negative consequences on a daily basis. These were not bottom line problems on a spreadsheet. These were interpersonal problems that sat in our office and looked us in the eye. #painful.

Over time, by embracing and implementing 360° Management, this state of unhealthy affairs has been mostly eradicated. With inner vision from trusted advisors, *above and below and alongside us*, our own weaknesses and ambivalences were exposed, and our true feelings about some difficult colleagues came out.

One thing that receiving 360° Management helped us see is this: When someone is failing in a role, you do a huge disservice to everyone involved by not addressing it. A person who is not thriving needs to be freed up to move to a place that is the right fit for them.

360° Management cuts through the morass of baked in hierarchies and gets everyone to the truth quicker.

> The difficulty lies not so much in developing
> new ideas as in escaping from old ones.
> —JOHN MAYNARD KEYNES, 1936

JUST OUR KIND

An inspiring living example of 360° work practices is taking place at KIND Snacks, the brainchild of Mexican-American businessman, philanthropist, and author Daniel Lubetzky. Established as "not-only-for-profit," the company's stated mission is "creating a kinder and healthier world—one act, one snack at a time."

It's working like gangbusters. At the time of this writing, KIND is the fastest-growing snack company in the United States, estimated to be valued at more than $4 billion.

At the heart of it all is Lubetzky, a powerful, confident visionary who might have started as a religious figure or a political leader under other circumstances. In fact, one of the reasons Lubetzky cuts such a striking figure in the movement toward compassionate business practices is that he didn't come straight from the business world per se. The son of a Holocaust-survivor and a Mexican Jew, Lubetzky's earliest efforts included a Haas Koshland Fellowship to write about ways Arabs and Israelis can foster peace through joint ventures. Describing himself as a "social entrepreneur working to build bridges between people," the rush of enormous success in the snack trade does not seem to have derailed his primary sense of purpose one bit. He continues to develop unusual hybrids between altruism and capital, most recently launching Empatico, a $20 million, multi-year initiative to broaden kids' worldviews through meaningful interactions with peers across the globe, and Feed the Truth, which seeks to improve public health by making truth, transparency, and integrity the foremost values in today's food system. In 2015, President Barack Obama and Commerce Secretary Penny Pritzker named Lubetzky a Presidential Ambassador for Global Entrepreneurship. He's also an appointee to the Anti-Defamation League's Inaugural Board of Directors.

Close, cooperative, interdependent—Lubetzky and his team embody the new age.

"It's very much an open meritocracy here," he says with pride. "I've seen many, many places that I actually admire overall, but that somehow just failed at creating an open culture. I know a person who is considered one of the best CEOs of all time, a very impressive person . . . but if you understand the culture in that company, nobody ever dares disagree with that CEO or whatever the CEO says. They won't confront the CEO because they know it's not going to end well. And it terrifies me to become that."

Lubetzky understands the paradoxes and pitfalls of late-era capitalism, and his self-scrutiny is one of his most 10x qualities. "The more you succeed," he told us, "the more you are engendered to thinking that you cannot make mistakes, that you're infallible, the more you intimidate people. It's not what I want."

With this in mind, he has built KIND on the bedrock of his values—transparency, honesty, ownership, and critical thinking. "I welcome disagreement," he says, "so one of the main things I try to do is create a culture where we foster critical thinking and critical listening. And we welcome feedback and we welcome people that say, *'I don't agree with you.'* And we don't do it as jerks. The people that I have the most trust in here are provocative to a point—not provocative for the sake of being provocative because that's annoying. But they're true critical thinkers, healthy skeptics."

To grow this "open air" environment, KIND stages team orientations that include quirky confessions from new and old team members—hidden life details people wouldn't figure out if they weren't told. At one recent powwow, a new team member confessed a secret phobia, which led to a group-wide discussion of phobias. "We all ended up sharing and getting closer, all of us."

For Lubetzky, this regular exercise isn't just about "meet and greet." It's an important watershed moment where every new hire is given permission and even actively encouraged to question everything and speak their mind. "It's so important that people recognize that this is *not* just a job, that we treat each other like family. Everybody is an equal in that room."

Obviously, the core of his mission is kindness, but for Lubetzky, kindness is not what many think. "A lot of people confuse kindness with weakness because they think being kind is synonymous with being *nice*." He says the word with just a tinge of disgust. "You can be nice and be passive, without anything pushing you to *do right*. Real kindness requires an action. You need to be a protagonist in your own story."

If it seems counterintuitive that a billion-dollar company can stand on such an ephemeral notion as kindness, Lubetzky is quick to explain that, seen from a certain angle, kindness is synonymous with proactive problem-solving. "A nice person often isn't willing to confront challenges, but a kind person, by definition, always at least *tries* to solves problems. A nice person just doesn't bully people; a kind person stands up to the bullies."

It's our observation that Lubetzky's vision of kindness in the workplace can only lead directly to 360° management—open culture, opinion sharing, honest expression, healthy feedback exchange, and mutual problem solving, all under an umbrella of genuine safety. Lubetzky agrees, but notes that it has been a learning curve for the company. The balance of kindness and accountability didn't happen overnight.

"Several years ago, we didn't meet our numbers," he recalls, "but they weren't bad, so I gave people bonuses anyway. And we created this environment where some people started expecting stuff—a culture of entitlement rather than the meritocracy we want to create. A lot of people started thinking that because we're 'kind,' nobody gets fired, nobody loses their bonus. Well, that doesn't work because people who perform exceptionally well need to be differentiated from those who don't. You need to create a culture of accountability, too. Without accountability, you're not being kind to anyone. And when you're not willing to provide feedback to someone because you think you're being nice, you're actually doing them a huge disservice."

Remarkably, KIND is even putting a new spin on the single most unpleasant work transaction there is: termination. They always have a reason for termination, and they always give team members a severance package beyond what's normally considered good, but what's most game changing (and most 10x) is the attitude they bring to the undertaking.

"We don't 'fire' people," Lubetzky says. "It doesn't mean that we don't let people go. It means we don't do it in a nasty way where you're shown the door. Of course, if somebody is criminal or they engage in sexual misconduct or they're racist or any of these horrible things, you immediately show them out because they're poisoning the well. But in most cases you need to remind yourself that *you brought these people*. And if things didn't work out, it's not only on them."

This is a humane and refreshing turnaround from the days when the pink slip was delivered with hasty cruelty, followed by the security guard. Often, KIND will even enlist the person who is being let go to help find and train a replacement. It's not "adios, amigo." It's "you're still family—and we still have your back."

"When someone has to be let go, we blame ourselves first," Lubetzky says. "And in fact, we have sometimes been slow to discover that a person just isn't right for the job we hired them for, that they're just not going to work out. That's on us, too. Everything you do is either strengthening or undermining the culture of kindness and accountability."

Conversely, if someone wants out, Lubetzky has learned to not go overboard trying to retain them. Part of being kind is letting people move on when their heart is no longer in it.

In pure 360° fashion, Lubetzky also doesn't ascribe to the culture of six-month or one-year reviews. He believes in giving and receiving immediate feedback, always constructive. "Great leaders seek feedback from all sides," he insists. "Because, in the end, it's the people you're bringing to your organization that define who you're going to become."

The goal for KIND team members, according to Lubetzky, is to experience "ownership," which he defines by two measures—the financial and the cultural. The financial is comprehensive. "Every full-time team member gets stock options. Everybody's an owner, regardless of your seniority. We have four-hundred-plus owners in KIND. Also, everybody's eligible for a bonus, and we have a long-term incentive cash program available to 100 percent of the organization, not just to senior members. There is no strata."

Cultural ownership is harder to define but no less mandatory. "Ownership of the company means encouraging people to express their opinions at every stage. We welcome challenges, and we honor people for being willing to question dogma and assumptions. And by isolating which assumptions are leading us, we solve a lot of our most difficult problems."

On one level, it's as if KIND treats each member of the team as a free-standing entrepreneur, with the ability to weigh in and seek guidance where it really counts, and the power to benefit from all the company's big successes. That it's working so well is something of a minor miracle and a testament to the power of multidirectional management and open culture. Lubetzky remains as dedicated as he is gregarious, and you can't help thinking that all of this couldn't have happened to a nicer guy.

"I never set out to become a wealthy person," he says. "That was never my driver. I wanted to have a positive impact, to build bridges. When I was a kid, nine years old, my dad started talking to me about what he went through in the Holocaust, being in a concentration camp, and it terrified me. He didn't pull any punches. But he also shared how people rose . . . to have courage at a moment when things were darkest. And kindness was the only reason he survived. One percent of people my dad's age survived the Holocaust because the Nazis didn't have use for children. But through kindness he survived and . . . it drove me to want to foster empathy and respect and humanity in one another. That's what's driven me, always. That's my true north."

HALLWAY MANAGEMENT

You may feel you already know Z100's Elvis Duran, and odds are you've heard him speak. A radio host since the early '80s, a Z100 host since 1989, and the morning show host since 1996, Duran is syndicated across roughly eighty stations as well as XM Satellite and the iHeartRadio app. At the time of this writing, *Elvis Duran and the Morning Show* is the most listened to Top 40 morning radio program in the United States, ranked #1 in nearly eighty markets. He's literally got our nation by the ears.

Still, when this titan of the airwaves shows up for work, he considers himself a single member of a synergistic, collegial team—a team with some very unorthodox habits. They eschew meetings and prefer to gab in the halls. They don't overplan. They have a little too much fun and truly enjoy one another's company. They ask one another smart and difficult questions. They have one another's backs.

If this sounds more like a hang-out than an actual business, keep in mind that every single weekday from 6:00 a.m. to 10:00 a.m. Eastern time, they put on a show that is engaging, multidimensional, and darn near seamless. Despite the fact that it's Duran's name on the marquee, he views the operation holistically.

"Here's the magical way our universe works," Duran explains. "To the people working with me, I make it very clear that I'm *not their boss*. Yes, at the end of the day, I'm the loudest guy there and, you know, I'll probably have a final say when it comes to many decisions. But I don't want them to think of me as someone on some other level. I have to perform *with* them, because, for four hours a day, we're on a stage together. And I can't reprimand people on the air. I cannot correct them. The best I can do is *motivate them as a friend*. And that philosophy has bled into our relationships off-mic as well."

A Texas native and a long-time New Yorker, Duran's signature talking style on and off the air is a warm blend of those two polarities—the easy drawl and the big city spiel. He discusses his workday with just a tinge of comical Southern country boy fatalism, marveling at the fact that it all seems to function despite the odds.

"Our room is really a free-for-all," he says. "People telling jokes, others trying to top them. But they all know their opinions are welcomed. They know I have a deep respect for what they bring to the table. And *I* know that I can't do what they do. I'd be lost without them."

Duran's door is always open to his staff, but surprisingly he prefers not to take his work home with him, and he's quick to point out that the free exchange of ideas and opinions is really just a byproduct of his personality. "It's not like we even cultivated an open atmosphere or anything that formal. We operate this way because I hate bullshit. I just don't like time-wasting. I'm not a firm believer in sitting down and having meetings, I don't like them. Let's just meet in the hall and, you know, *'What do you think about this?' 'Great, let's do it.' 'Go!'*"

What Duran is describing is 360° Management in full swing, a machine where all parts are free to communicate with each other. Incredibly, he and his team don't even really plan their four hour shows, other than the prep work necessary to properly accommodate a guest or develop a brand-new segment. They discovered, through painstaking trial and error, that too much prep undermines the flow. "When we showed up Friday morning, we found out we were no longer in a Thursday night mood."

Naturally, this policy of winging it can sometimes scare the bejeezus out of the top brass at corporate.

"They'll ask what tomorrow's show will be like and I'll say, 'I don't know!' And it's like, 'What kind of business model is that?!'" Duran laughs. "But it keeps my team fresh because we trust each other, we trust that the ideas are there, and we trust that we'll listen to each other about what works and what doesn't. And you know what? We end up with enough material every morning to do ten shows."

In a brilliant act of managing up, Duran understands and respects corporate's concerns, and so, to compensate, he has honed his team to become almost entirely self-sufficient, a kind of high-functioning island. "Corporate entities are running around putting out fires all day," he says. "I do what I can to not be a fire."

As with Lubetzky and KIND bars, it's notable that the holistic nature of the product itself seems to affect relations between the workers in a healthy way. The shared sense of mission has the power to transform the very people who deliver the goods. Duran and his team observed a giant spike in ratings when they did shows that involved motivational speaking—encouraging people to get out there and improve their lives and relationships—but they also found their own communication was improved. Connecting your team to the *values* of the mission is a key game changer in the new workplace.

"Just by virtue of speaking about the positives in life and motivating people on the air," Duran says, "it motivates the management team as well. In our room, it's almost as if we have our staff meeting live for four hours every day."

As Duran puts it, his people are in "the friendship business. People are in their cars and on their way to work, either leaving a bad relationship in the bed behind them or going into a bad relationship with a boss. They need someone they can trust for 20 minutes to an hour every day."

It's working—for Duran, his listeners, and his organization. As with Springsteen's team, longevity is something to behold—Duran boasts of five employees who've been with him for twenty-five years, an anomaly in the nomadic world of radio. He also makes it a point to support ex-staff, long after they've moved on. He also talks about his employees—from the sound engineers to the administrators and beyond—with a sense of real awe and respect.

At one point, Duran had the itch to be a program director himself, to "architect" the sound of a radio station, but the formal role of manager tripped him up. "Overseeing people was not my thing, I'd never done it before and I hated it. I hated getting calls in the middle of the night from people telling me they were too drunk to show up to work, I didn't like that kind of responsibility. But I learned from it."

Duran returned to the mic at Z100 with a renewed sense of purpose. When David Katz, formerly of the Don Buchwald & Associates (Howard Stern, Kathleen Turner, et al.) approached him with a vision for syndicating the show, Duran was intrigued. Z100 balked at the idea, and in true 10x fashion, he and Katz decided to do it themselves. The show spread like a wildfire and the inevitable followed: his team grew, and teams need to be managed. This time, Duran deployed a 360° managerial style.

"I've learned to love it," Duran explains, "because the truth is, my team manages *me*, more than the other way around. They know what makes me tick. I didn't get into radio because it's a business. I got into radio because it's *not* a business to me. I was an awkward, bratty kid, I didn't want to be a boy scout, I couldn't play baseball. But I had that need to connect with people and communicate. My dad was a big storyteller, joking, fun-loving, *drinking-bourbon-at-5-o'clock-every-day-and-telling-jokes-to-his-friends* kind of guy. I wanted to be that. Radio taught me how to actually communicate with people, so every time I think of it as a business I kind of retreat a little bit, and whoever is managing me needs to always understand that in order to get a better return."

TURNING ON YOUR MANAGERIAL COMPASS

In both of the above examples, what you're seeing is a game changing blueprint from the top which dictates the tone with which an entire organization runs. Fundamentally, for 360° Management to truly work, it has to start from the top down.

Still, there are plenty of things you can do, below, adjacent, and above you, to help improve the environment within your corporate structure. 360° Management is the 5D version of what we talked about in Chapter 3 when we first discussed *manageability*. You might think of it as manageability in the round. This panoramic view is crucial—in order to be a 10xer, you need to be open to learning, willing to seek advice, and, most of all, be adept at two-way communication—and *not* just between you and superiors.

You need to seek guidance *everywhere*.

When feedback is not proffered, you go get it, from as many credible sources as possible. And you need to be okay with it even when it hurts. Especially when it hurts.

Time and time again, we have noticed that, in the face of criticism, the true 10xer never gets angry or defensive, never tells you why your observations are untrue, and most of all they never, ever pass the buck. The true 10xer says, "Thank you. I didn't realize I was doing that. Can you tell me a little more so I can better understand and correct course?" Curiosity rules this roost.

Conversely, those who are unmanageable, who will never become 10xers, will usually tend to have communication problems with *everyone*—bosses, juniors, peers, at home. So how do you deal with somebody who is not 10x, but who *thinks* they are? It ain't easy. Even if an unmanageable talent generates lots of money for a brief period of time, their relationship to the venture will ultimately be unsustainable because they won't allow themselves to deploy 360° Management. The result is that the unmanageable talent has refused to investigate their own weak spots, refused to connect meaningfully with others, and refused to offer their advice where others need it most.

At the core, what the 10xer understands is that self-improvement is the best use of their time, money, and energy. There is no better investment. Still, trying to pull off self-improvement without a sense of just who is above, below, and beside you can leave even the best-intentioned talent stabbing in the dark, making wild guesses about where they need help the most. Once a talent embraces 360° Management, they create the space for rapid evolution.

360° Management is not an insta-cure, and every situation calls for its own finessing. Still, here are a few commonly recurring workplace challenges, and some 360° directions for how you might handle them.

Scenario #1: Managing Sideways

GOAL: "I want to get more credit for my work and acknowledgment. Currently it is rare."

SCENARIO: "I am doing really good work but rarely being recognized."

ACTION: First, check with others to make sure you're actually doing decent work. Most coworkers will be honest if they know you're open to the truth. Then, enroll a colleague to be your champion in exchange for being theirs.

STEPS:

1. Identify the right partner given the options.
2. Get away from the office with them to have a candid conversation.
3. Explain the nature and value of the Third Party Effect.
4. Ask if they are willing for the two of you to become each other's cheerleaders and advocates, offering each other accolades in front of fellow employees whenever appropriate and possible.
5. Make absolutely sure they are comfortable enough to say no if this offer is not right for them. You don't want to cut this deal only to find out they don't like you or your work.
6. Adjust as you go to make sure neither of you are doing too much or too little.

PITFALLS:

1. You may not be doing really good work, in which case this will be a tough sell.
2. If your approach is too blatant and obvious, the others at work will understand that this praise was "paid for."
3. You may choose someone who rarely does good work, in which case your own credibility is in danger of taking a hit from backing the wrong horse.
4. You may do a great job promoting them, and they bail on you and don't reciprocate. It happens.

Scenario #2: Managing Up

GOAL: "I need to get better at what I do and need more feedback to do it."

SCENARIO: "I am ambitious and want to continue growing and improving toward 10xness. My company does semi-annual reviews, but they are not enough and are not taken seriously. These reviews seem to be an exercise in 'checking the box.'"

ACTION: Enroll your supervisor in helping you achieve this goal.

STEPS:
1. Assess the landscape and try to identify any potential obstacles.
2. Send a note to your boss that says:

Dear first name,
I really hope you don't mind this formal note, but I wanted to enlist your help, and I wanted to ask for it in the most respectful and carefully thought out manner possible. My desire to grow and improve in my role here is tremendous and your guidance has been very helpful thus far.

As such, I wanted to see if I could enlist a bit of help from you, since our wagons are somewhat hitched and the better I do, the better it is for our whole team.

With that in mind, do you think you would be willing to provide additional feedback for me in one or all of the following ways:

Real time, i.e. whenever you see that I'm doing something good or bad, please be sure to let me know, and definitely tell me how I can make improvements.

Monthly, i.e. a quick 15-30 minute sit down each month where we review my work and discuss places where there is room for improvement.

Quarterly . . . Same as Monthly but less frequent
Thank you for your time and consideration. Please don't hesitate if
you have any questions or concerns.

3. Assess your boss's response and adjust accordingly. If it was positive, make sure to calendar and make it easy for them to follow through.

PITFALLS: Boss says, "Not a chance." Fallback position might be if they were willing to give you emails or notes in lieu of a sit-down. If it's really a dead-end, you could ask the same from a peer in exchange for doing the same for them.

Boss says, "Yes," but then never takes the time to do it.

Boss doesn't even respond.

Scenario #3: Managing Up Revisited

GOAL: "I want to get a raise and promotion."

SCENARIO: "I believe I have done good work, I have had positive feedback from my superior and positive results in hitting my goals. However, there's been no reward for this thus far."

ACTION: Enroll your supervisor in helping you achieve this goal.

STEPS:
1. Assess the landscape and look for any obstacles.
2. Send a note to your boss that says:

Dear first name:
I hope you are doing well and I hope you don't mind this formal

note, but I wanted to enlist your help and wanted to ask for it in the most respectful and carefully thought out manner.

As you know, I have (list all your great accomplishments, your time at the company, your love for the work, and any other positive, company-related actions, including mentoring people, meeting goals, breaking records, making sales, etc.).

Because of this and all of your positive feedback in and out of my reviews, it is my fundamental belief (and hope) that these contributions have reflected well on you, me, and the rest of the team. I know we all sink or swim together, so supporting one another is something I value above almost all else. I know you know and believe this too, which is why I am writing to ask for your assistance in helping me make a meaningful improvement to my comp and my position. I believe if it were up to you, this would be easy, but since there are others involved, I am really hoping you would advocate on my behalf. In addition to your seniority and leadership, it is always better having someone else sing your praises. Even saying what I did in the first paragraph was uncomfortable for me.

Assuming you are amenable to this, is there anything I can provide to make this easier? I will gladly do all the heavy lifting.

Thanks for your time and attention, and please don't hesitate if you have any questions or comments.

3. Follow up at regular intervals until you get a response.

PITFALLS: Your boss doesn't agree with your assessment. If this is the case, you might ask for the hard feedback so you know: A. How you got it so wrong and B. What is needed to get to the point where you can try again.

Your boss agrees but there are other obstacles (such as budget cuts, his boss doesn't care, the company is in trouble, etc.).

Scenario #4: Managing Diagonally

GOAL: "I want to support a member or members of my team that are below me, though I may or may not be their manager."

SCENARIO: "I know that a supportive environment helps with job satisfaction and overall performance, and I want to be a part of making my workplace supportive by encouraging and going to bat for those below me on my team. I also know our wagons are hitched so I want to help them succeed as it will be beneficial to our whole group."

ACTION:
1. Get to know the members of my team who are below me.
2. Determine those members that are really fantastic and then sing their praises.
3. For those who are not quite as developed, give them guidance and support where feasible.

BYPRODUCT: Leading by example will hopefully be contagious and other members of your team will behave the same way, either by singing your praises or singing the praises and/or mentoring those below them.

PITFALLS: It's feasible you back a bad horse and someone whom you are singing the praises of either does something bad, or doesn't reciprocate with you when they are in a position to do so. Obviously backing a bad horse won't win you any favor with your supervisor, but don't let that alone prevent you from continuing to champion and mentor those beneath you who are deserving. Karmic points are won in all circumstances.

MINI-SCENARIOS

HOW TO ...	WHAT YOU MIGHT SAY
Thank those who give you feedback.	*While some of that was hard to hear, I am so appreciative that you took the time to share this with me. As you know, I really want to grow and improve and your input is invaluable. Please keep it coming as frequently and directly as possible. I can handle it.*
Ask for positive feedback if it hasn't been offered alongside negative feedback.	*Thanks so much for your input. While that was very hard to hear, it will be helpful for me in making improvements. I know that I will learn much more from this kind of constructive criticism than I will from anything on the plus side, but I was curious if there are any areas where you feel I am excelling or have made any meaningful improvements. This info will help me better understand what is working well and should be supported. Thanks so much for this.*
Work with your supervisor to come up with a plan to improve when negative feedback is given.	*This feedback was wonderful and I really want to make improvements to eliminate the deficiencies you identified. Toward that end, I was wondering if you could help me with planning some action steps and goals toward improvement.*
Present ideas up the food chain in the right way, by knowing your audience, and by understanding the nuances of how they will react.	Note: You have to know your superior. If they are someone who can really share the wealth, then you can be much more direct and simply raise your idea directly:

HOW TO . . .	WHAT YOU MIGHT SAY
Present ideas up the food chain in the right way, by knowing your audience, and by understanding the nuances of how they will react. *(cont.)*	*I was just struck with an idea about how to do/improve/make X, and I would love the opportunity to sit down with you and present it. I really think it could make a meaningful change for Y.* Conversely, if your superior is one of those people for whom everything needs to be their idea, you might try something more like this: *Something you said, inspired an idea about how to do/improve/make X, and I would love the opportunity to sit down with you and present it. I really think it could make a meaningful change for Y.*
Approach feedback with curiosity rather than defensiveness.	*Really? I wasn't aware that I was doing that, but I am really eager to hear and learn more about your experience so I can work on improving.*
Create the right opportunities to talk about your goals with superiors.	*I know we don't often get to have meta conversations about my role here, but I was wondering if we could carve out a little time to discuss how I might better reach the goals you've set for me, and in turn advance my career. Part of what I am hoping for in this conversation is your guidance on how I can better help and advance things for you.*
Know how to disagree.	Start by restating the item that you would like to disagree with, so you can confirm that you actually understand what is being proposed. Once that is confirmed, go with the positive and negative.

HOW TO . . .	WHAT YOU MIGHT SAY
Know how to disagree. (cont.)	So if I understand this correctly, you are proposing X, which would do/operate/etc. by Y. Is that correct? Okay. Given that I seem to understand correctly, while I like A, B, or C about that concept, there are a few issues that concern me. Are you open to hearing about these concerns?
Provide feedback up the chain.	I had an experience I want to chat with you about, and I wonder if you would be open to my giving some candid feedback. 1) I know we have not known each other long, but I feel our rapport is such that I can share this with you, but only with your explicit permission. or 2) Given the history and strength of our relationship, I am confident you would want to hear this but only with your explicit permission.
Understand that peers and subordinates can be just as effective for providing feedback as superiors.	I am humbly and strongly requesting your feedback. We have a lot of contact on an ongoing basis and I am really focused on learning more about my weaknesses, blind spots, or other areas that need meaningful improvement. My goals are to: 1. Learn what I don't know about myself that you do (see the top left quadrant of Johari Window) 2. Find means and methods to improve myself. 3. Set goals for myself based on #1 and #2. Thank you so much for taking the time to do this as it is incredibly important to me.

HOW TO . . .	WHAT YOU MIGHT SAY
Create organization from chaos when your leader or boss won't.	*Given these goals, would it be reasonable to set up a tactical plan for achieving them? With your blessing, I would love to create a spreadsheet/timeline/project management tool/document/etc. to align on who is doing what and by when, so we can all be working toward the same goals as a team. Would that be acceptable and useful for us?*
Request success metrics when they are not provided.	*I am really excited to do what is requested, but I would love to gain a little more clarity about what success looks like. Are there some measurable goals we could add to this endeavor so I can be sure I am doing what is needed and doing it well? If the goals are not yet clear, I would be happy to work with you to come up with and clarify them, but most important, I want a way to measure my performance as I know this is a meaningful task.*
Always go the extra mile.	This should be obvious, but the most successful people are successful for a reason. Where others shy away from work or look for shortcuts, they don't. Volunteer for the harder work. Be willing to help coworkers with projects. In short, be the person that everyone else can count on to get the job done. *Given what you have laid out as the objectives for this, I wanted to go the extra mile and complete X. Before doing so, I just wanted to confirm that this is acceptable and would be a positive move on my part. Please let me know. Thanks.*

HOW TO . . .	WHAT YOU MIGHT SAY
Never assume.	We've said it a bunch in this book, but communication is the cornerstone of any success. Never assume someone knows what you know and never assume someone is going to do something. Be clear, overstate, and overcommunicate until such a time that you know your teammates and superiors well enough to know what things need to be spelled out and what things don't. *Thanks for giving me the instructions. I think I understand what is needed to complete X but just want to clarify to be doubly sure. Could you please confirm that when you said X, that meant Y. Please let me know and I will get started. Thanks.*
Never shy away from delivering bad news.	Failures and successes both teach us things. Still, the fact of human nature is that we're more prone to quickly announce a success and hide a failure. When something isn't working, don't wait, communicate. You'll gain the respect of your superiors and colleagues and gain a reputation as someone who steps up when things are tough. Whenever possible, try to surround the bad news with good news as well; it always helps the recipient absorb the news more effectively.

HOW TO . . .	WHAT YOU MIGHT SAY
Never shy away from delivering bad news. (cont.)	*Hi All,* *I have some bad news and a bit of good news. I hate to be the bearer of this and certainly hope you won't shoot the messenger but given X, we are going to come up short on Y. Here are the reasons for this and while I wish there was another possibility we feel like we have looked at it from all sides with this being the best option.* *The good news is: We caught this early, we learned from this mistake, we will save time or money, the product will be better, the team has come together to redouble our efforts and now we can mitigate this to avoid further damage.*
Ask for help.	When you're new to a company or team, ask as many questions as possible. Your instinct may be to try and figure things out on your own. Don't. Everyone has been in your shoes, everyone has been the new person. Once you settle in, only then should you try to figure out solutions. But even seasoned employees reach out for help and guidance when they encounter unfamiliar roadblocks. A sure sign that the culture of your company is poor is if you don't feel comfortable asking questions. *I am sorry if the questions I am asking in this email are common knowledge here, but I would much rather be doubly cautious than start out with a blunder. As such, here are a few questions which will help me get started and deliver the right results . . .*

In our next chapter, we'll take a look at matters from both sides at once. We'll explore what it means to sometimes be the manager and sometimes the talent. And we'll reveal the absolute necessity of getting good at both.

TAKEAWAYS FROM CHAPTER 8

- A culture of support, openness, and safety is synonymous with 360° Management, where those above you protect you and give you the latitude to express your ideas in full; those adjacent to you need to feel sufficiently empowered to help you and receive help from you; and those beneath you are emboldened to offer you support and come to you with their ideas, challenges, and disasters.
- In essence, 360° Management is about turning your managers, your peers, and your underlings into the great managers we've described in this book.
- Not every person has the tools, training, or the proclivity to be great at management. That's why taking an active role in the flow of managerial guidance both to and from you is a form of taking responsibility for your own destiny.
- *No management* is definitely not the answer, and *less management* is frequently not the answer either. 360° Management means flexibility and agility flowing in all directions.
- To be a 10xer, you need to be open to learning, willing to seek advice, and, most of all, adept at two-way communication—and *not* just between you and superiors.
- The manageable talent, finally, understands that the best use of their time and energy is self-improvement, and 360° Management is a fast track to getting there.

1 2 3 4 5 6 7 8 **9** 10

THE ULTIMATE SKILL—
DONNING THE DOUBLE HAT

There are no superheroes, just us.
We are the ones we've been waiting for.
—SHIZA SHAHID, MALALA FUND, 2013

D o you see yourself as the talent or as the management?

Whatever your answer, you're only half right.

Today, we are living in a Double-Hat World, where everyone, no matter how seasoned, no matter how skilled, must learn to speak the language and adopt the skills of the other side. Perceptually, this is a learning curve that's harder for some than others, but it's an essential one in the stream-lined, do-more-with-less world we live in now.

As we've aimed to demonstrate, the contemporary workplace is not re-ally a place at all, but a state of workflow with a code of conduct that is virtually unreadable to previous generations. With the quickening disinte-gration of the old hierarchical employee/employer model, it's become cru-cial that people see themselves as talent at least some of the time. It's equally important that people recognize they are managers some of the time—with a genuine responsibility to give praise and guidance where it's needed, and to pick up the reins and lead at times. There's just no other way.

For dyed-in-the-wool managers, even those rare leaders who've been overseeing the same department for twenty-plus years, switching hats means developing the ability to reframe yourself as talent when the situation calls for it. Your team might be a hundred people strong, but unless you're the CEO, you still have people above you whom you'll need on your side to help you advance *your* career. That's why you need to periodically take off your manager hat, put on your talent hat, and ask yourself some big questions: Am I getting the support I need to advance? Do I have clear personal and professional goals? Are my supervisors and colleagues giving me the praise I deserve and the feedback I need to improve? Are my direct reports communicating openly with me? Do I still have room for advancement or do I need to make a move in order to achieve my big picture goals?

In the absence of the right answers, you can't lead effectively because you are not taking care of your own needs effectively. And if your own needs aren't being met, what steps can you take to change your situation? Is it time to look for new opportunities? Have you exhausted all potential options internally and externally?

As a manager, you always need the support of others in your sphere or you'll be, literally and figuratively, on an island all alone. This is especially true when your own manager is not a great one. Taking the manager hat off and putting the talent hat on is the quickest way to see what life is like for your superiors, your colleagues, and your direct reports.

We've also aimed to prove in this book that no talent can make it without strong management looking out for them. Only an outside entity can give you the balanced skin-in-the-game and third party POV you need to understand what forces are truly at play around you.

For even the greatest talents, your primary skill set is never enough. In addition to being a strong practitioner, as we pointed out in the prior chapter, you'll need to provide great management to the surprising number of people whose careers you have a stake in. In the old school corporation, you stayed in your lane. Today, with smaller teams being responsible for a much wider zone of activity, your every action has a ripple effect on company culture. Moreover, learning how to be that outside POV for someone else is the only way to really know how strong management actually works.

We imagine that most employees, managers included, don't really consider themselves talent, but it's time for a rethink across the board. Managers are indeed talent, even when they're *not* changing roles or looking for a new job. When you frame yourself as talent, it can cause a dramatic shift in your own perception—not only of yourself and your value to the organization, but also in the way you approach other members of your team, below, adjacent, and above you.

To be a talent is to acknowledge your own importance in the scheme of things.

Adopting this attitude also plays a critical role when deciding who to seek out and partner up with for your career. Nothing could be more important.

If people simply define themselves in the narrow confines of *employee* or *manager*, they may not take the same steps that *talent* would in a number of crucial ways—by surrounding themselves with credible advocates; by taking it upon themselves to constantly learn and grow; by supporting fellow team members and managing 360°; by embracing all the elements that make for a 10xer.

Most importantly, when people realize that they are both talent and management, they can start to empathize with the multitude of challenges on the other side.

THE OTHER HAT: TRAGEDIES AND TRIUMPHS

You'll never be 10x until you're comfortable donning "the other hat."

If you hold dear an image of yourself as primarily the talent or primarily the management, switching hats will likely not come easily. This is especially true for those who have followed their natural proclivities, and groomed themselves to be one or the other, a process that often starts at a very early age.

However, if you cling to either identity, you pay a price.

A fellow artist manager recently recounted a story to us about one of his most accomplished music clients. Let's call him "Billy." As Billy was really hitting his stride, his team was growing quickly. At home, he was surrounded by managers, agents, label people, international promoters, publicists, lawyers, and accountants, all attending to his every whim. He was the Talent with a capital T.

The problem was, out there on tour, Billy had to roll with a different growing team—a highly skilled road crew and a band of top-tier musicians. These people were talents in their own right, and they were an essential part of his rigorous touring life, day in and day out. They required a different level of care and attention than Billy's entourage back home.

What Billy needed to do was switch hats and, for the first time ever, act as a manager. Unfortunately, at that early stage of his career, leadership was not his forte.

Before we describe the missteps, we need to have Billy's management take some ownership and point out the fact that, as members of Billy's management team back home, it was their job to prepare him and train him for managing a team of his own. No matter how you slice it, that was a mistake made by and owned by them.

Almost as soon as Billy hit the road, he made a variety of mistakes, most of them too mundane to report, but the gist is, he just didn't think guiding or helping others was his responsibility. Of all the situations Billy mishandled, the worst might be the time he fired one of his best friends and longtime original band member via a crew member intermediary, with no real warning or explanation. This was not a situation where the person had done something wrong. Billy just didn't want him around anymore. The impact of Billy's poorly handled firing was brutal on morale for those who were still on his touring team, and the spiritual cost of this one incident was immeasurable. By sowing so much doubt within his own crew, he was like a general who had betrayed his country.

Yes, the manager had no idea he was planning to terminate anyone, but he should have. Billy's communication skills were not highly developed at this young age. Still, the manager should have taught Billy how to manage *before* he made bad decisions. Not to relentlessly pick on that other manager, we have made virtually identical mistakes along the way. They (and we) should have seen that, even though he had managers of his own, he had not yet absorbed important lessons on how to be one. This is a key fact of the Double-Hat World: Nobody, no matter how talented, can afford to *not* think like a manager.

Part of what tripped Billy up, obviously, was his ego. He saw himself as a talent (read: star) and viewed the work of helping his team as a petty nuisance. This kind of thinking will always eventually come back to bite you, because the more successful you become, the more you will certainly have people to manage. As the organization grows, those people you are managing have more and bigger responsibilities. Recognizing this is key.

Thinking back on Billy's situation, Dr. Jeffrey R. Solomon, whom you met in Chapter 4, sheds some much needed light. He quotes Lao Tzu who once said, "A leader is best when people barely know he exists, when his work is done, his aim fulfilled, they will say: we did it ourselves."

As Dr. Solomon explains: "Managers who understand Lao Tzu's concept are able to swing back and forth between production and pure management with little difficulty. When you aren't concerned with taking credit, the flow of work allows for the manager to make substantive contributions along with the line worker and to see others take ownership of those contributions."

Had Billy inspired his team to pull off and take credit for a great tour, they would have stood by him for the next one and the next. Had he prepared for the eventual blowback of a difficult firing, his team might have empathized with him, rather than vilified him. By setting himself apart, Billy alienated himself from his own team. He turned himself into the enemy.

Another story, this time from the tech side: A high-level developer we represented named Gabe had to make the switch from being an individual contributor to team leader. Gabe had done a stint at Google working under some pretty good bosses, but he'd never really seen the kind of soft skills that make for stellar team leadership. The only semblance of managerial experience he had was acquired during the few months he worked as a freelancer with us.

Still, Gabe had one thing going for him that Billy didn't: He understood that he really had no choice, he *wanted* to learn to lead, and he was hungry to find out what it took to lead well. He had tackled most of what was involved in being a great individual contributor and like most 10xers, he needed his next challenge and soon. 10xers rarely stay static long. Before long, he landed a prime role heading up a dev team at a recently funded start-up.

Gabe sought guidance from us, read books, watched videos, and asked others. He wanted to be just as 10x in managing his team as he was writing code. Despite the pressures of learning various new skills literally on the job, and despite some minor bumps in the road, Gabe successfully hired and inspired a group of fellow programmers to meet and beat challenging deadlines. Naturally, Gabe's higher-ups were thrilled with the transformation—he justified their faith. His desire to do well, combined with his willingness to work hard, persevere through adversity, and seek out and take guidance, made the transition from talent to manager a relatively seamless one. Today, he's an outstanding top-level manager/team leader and a 10x coder, leaning on fellow team leaders on the rare occasions that he needs extra guidance or feedback.

In some ways, the ability to act as a managerial force for others is the final test for any given talent. Even those 10xers who are individual contributors by choice still need to interact in ways that require management skills. There's just no getting around the need for two hats.

The great news is, by *being* the manager for someone whose career you genuinely care about, you are receiving a hands-on education in what constitutes *receiving* strong management. The better you can manage, the better you can *be* managed. You'll begin to know the shape and shade of good advice—how it's proffered and what it sounds like. You'll develop antennae for the Success and Sabotage Impulses. You'll be able to build trust by conveying your skin in the game. You'll experience the power of the Third Party Effect firsthand, and we're willing to bet you'll develop a craving for having a third party of your own, advocating for you in the clinch. Armed with the tools of management, you'll learn just how to get your own needs as a talent met.

DOUBLE-HAT FEEDBACK

To complicate matters, management must always be 360°, as we described in the previous chapter. It's no easy feat managing in all directions, while simultaneously team-building with those who report to you, *and* being a talent with your own "action skills" operating full force. Communicating effectively and constructing mutually agreed-upon goals will set the stage for positive growth, but nobody gets there without knowing how to don both hats.

In Chapter 5, we spoke with Michael Counts, an extremely gifted designer/director best known for his immersive theatrical work. He's also a prolific entrepreneur who spins businesses up with the speed of a cyclone. Counts is a fabulous exemplar of the strength of the Double Hat in daily life.

To give just one example of how adept he is at managing and being managed, Counts came to our office one day with a single goal in mind: He wanted to provide feedback to us—about the feedback we were giving him! With complete candor, he let us know that he needed our comments delivered in a manner very different from the way we were handling it.

At first, we were shocked. It was jarring to us when he said, "I feel like all you do is criticize," but we knew we were talking to somebody who understands strong management.

Our initial response, which was slightly defensive, was that we thought he could handle it. After all, Counts presents like a formidable business person. He can negotiate with the best of them, he's built complex business models, he understands virtually every financing structure out there, and he's totally unafraid of going head to head with some pretty tough characters.

Still, we forgot one thing: He might look like a businessperson, but in his soul, Counts is first and foremost a creative artist. He just happens to be that even rarer talent that also has incredibly strong business acumen. That personality type typically requires more encouragement and for good reason. They're up against the skeptics of the world. With each new innovative project, he has thousands of people telling him why it won't work.

In true 10x fashion, Counts made a direct request for more positive affirmation, and because he deserved it (and we know it to be a best practice), we didn't hesitate. He knew how to "manage his managers." That's the Double Hat in action.

The subject of "how much praise is enough" or "how much criticism is too much" is a complex one. An article in *Harvard Business Review* by Jack Zenger and Joseph Folkman called "The Ideal Praise-to-Criticism Ratio"[1] concluded that 5.6 positive comments for every negative one is the way to go. This startling imbalance might sound comical if it weren't based on solid academic research, conducted by Emily Heaphy and Marcial Losada. Examining sixty strategic-business-unit leadership teams at a large information-processing company, Heaphy and Losada discovered that the ratio of positive to negative remarks made an enormous difference between the most and least successful teams. The lowest-performing teams had a ratio of 0.36 to 1, in other words, almost three criticisms for every instance of praise.

An interesting "side conclusion" from the study is that a little negative feedback goes a long way. "Negative feedback is important when we're heading over a cliff," Zenger and Folkman write. "But even the most well-intentioned criticism can rupture relationships and undermine self-confidence and initiative. It can change behavior, certainly, but it doesn't cause people to put forth their best efforts."

Regarding feedback, the 10xer donning two hats is capable of two great feats. On the one hand, he or she is able to absorb and learn from a greater-than-average amount of criticism. On the other hand, he or she can deeply understand and respect the fact that people need praise just to function.

THE CHANGELING SOCIETY

One of the key reasons being able to switch hats is so important nowadays is the rapid rate of change across industries, caused in no small part by digitization. Where there is instability, there is a heightened need for flexibility.

First and foremost, the company that has your back today may not even exist tomorrow. Should you find yourself out of a gig, you'll be forced to reframe yourself as talent when you enter the open market. This is true even if what you're most talented at is management.

Second, a new tradition of doing more with less has taken hold of the contemporary workplace. Smaller work teams with greater responsibilities have to deliver more, faster, and with smoother synergy. This means that every practitioner, no matter how much they enjoy their alone time, will have to work with and manage others.

To add to the general atmosphere of transience, at the time of writing this book, there are approximately 750,000 open tech jobs. Contrast this with the jarring fact that colleges are only graduating approximately 56,000 students with computer science degrees, a number that has grown by a mere 7 percent in the last five years. As Quartz reports, there are "almost 10 times more US computing jobs open right now than there were students who graduated with computer science degrees"[2]—a peculiar statistic when you note that computer science is the highest-paid college degree for new employees, with a median base salary of $70,000.[3] The influx of talent from overseas is not much larger—H1B visa quotas hover around 65,000 persons max,[4] and when the cap is reached, the gates are closed. What all this amounts to is a massive supply-demand imbalance in the marketplace for tech talent, and a general imbalance in the larger work sphere.

The future doesn't look much more stable. The website Technically reports that, by 2025, the United States will have as many as 3.5 million STEM jobs available. "Jobs like computer science engineers, research scientists and information technology specialist will be in huge demand. However, two million of those jobs may go unfilled due to lack of qualified candidates."[5]

Not everyone we spoke with expressed unbridled enthusiasm for switching hats from talent to manager and back again, but everyone recognized the need for it, especially those interviewees who spring from the tech world.

Supercoder Bryan Bishop, whom you met in Chapter 7, says: "The truth is, I see myself mainly as talent. I can manage and lead others, but I really prefer to do that only if I am also in the trenches applying myself through programming." Bishop admits to sometimes missing the thrill of just programming, all day every day. "It's so relaxing to have a problem and apply your intellect to that problem in a very direct way."

Still, because much of Bishop's work involves architecture, planning, team management, code review, and security review—all activities that require the overseeing of others—he has no choice, he knows that management is part of the equation. He's really grown to embrace it.

Sam Brotherton, another supercoder we introduced you to in Chapter 1, sees the two roles as being somewhat intertwined. "The companies that I usually work with, they don't want me to have to actively *manage* someone, and they aren't hiring me to manage. But if I'm hired as a consultant, and I see people building something that hasn't worked for five other companies I've worked for, I'm going to speak up. That's part of the value add I bring to the table."

Jason Rubenstein, the CTO and Python/DevOps maven we also met in our first chapter, agrees with Brotherton. "In almost every engagement I've been on," Rubenstein says, "I've been asked to both write code *and* manage. This is probably correlated to the *diving save* nature of most of the engagements I get sent on."

A "diving save" in baseball describes a sudden move at the very last moment to "save the game." What Jason is describing is the chronic way a company will hire inexpensive and inexperienced tech talent, creating a product that won't work, is broken, or can't be shipped. In the ninth inning, these companies may finally turn to the 10xers, not only for their coding skills but for the managing acumen they bring to team environments.

Even outside the strictly tech realm, our interviewees seemed to have an uncanny, automatic grasp of the Double-Hat concept.

When Jesse Lee, the youth market maven we met in Chapter 2, puts on his management hat, he makes sure he doesn't bite off more than he can chew. "You can't really manage *everybody* right," he told us. "If I can manage five people effectively, they can manage five each, and so on. Then you have a scalable model where people really know who they're dealing with."

One way to look at all this is that management in general, and the management of talent specifically, is an artform that is coming into its own renaissance. These days, everyone—even CEOs and founders of megacorporations—are working with coaches to help them with management strategy. Managers at the highest level understand that they themselves need management too.

For A-Plan Coaching's co-founder and CEO Sara Ellis Conant, whom we met in Chapter 5, the talent of coaching mirrors the art of managing because they both come down to one thing: black-belt listening. "A good coach and a good manager both have to *begin* from the same starting point when they face their clients or employees. *'Tell me about yourself. Tell me what's important to you. Tell me what your career objectives are. Tell me how you like to be supported.'*"

Many of the heavy hitters we spoke with have, on their own, arrived at the same conclusion: being able to switch hats is the fast lane to excellence.

Jon Landau can manage the biggest rock star in the world, but at the end of the day, he leans on a handful of key people to give him guidance. Daniel Lubetzky may run a billion-dollar snack company, but he still takes the time to rigorously investigate his own management practices. Elvis Duran might have an agent that negotiates his deals and a boss at iHeart Radio to whom he answers, but when he interfaces with his own team, he knows that *his* management style will set the tone.

Each one of these game changers wears both hats and wears them well. The fact that their careers have such a strong impact is a testament to how well they pull it off.

Moreover, when they speak about their colleagues—business partners, clients, employees, and peers—they do so with full respect for their talents and their ability to guide. To see yourself both ways is to see the other party both ways, too.

> The pessimist complains about the wind.
> The optimist expects it to change.
> The leader adjusts the sails.
> —JOHN MAXWELL

RISING TIDES RAISE ALL BOATS

The beauty of the Double-Hat World is that it actually creates a triple winning affect. When you manage the people beneath you effectively, they get better, and when they get better, you do, too, so the whole team flourishes. Simultaneously, when you manage the people above you to help them manage you better, they become better managers and thereby help you and the rest of the people on your team become even better.

We don't mean to sound glib or overly idealistic. It's simply a proven fact that the whole team rises together as a result of strong, invested, compassionate, and goal-oriented management. When everybody is working hard to help those around them, those above them, and those beneath them, achievement kicks into a higher gear. As the old adage goes, rising tides raise all boats, and strong management buoys all talents.

Take the case of Cathy, a manager at a global digital marketing agency. Having spent her whole year wondering how she could better optimize her team and advance the company, she finally hit a wall. Lucky for her, she worked at a forward-thinking company that had arranged for a leadership coach to give its managers and key senior contributors some one-on-one guidance. Through this process, she came to some realizations. "I wasn't getting anywhere," she told us. "I realized I just needed to stop and take a big breath and do a little strategic planning for myself."

What Cathy was wisely enacting was the switch to her talent hat. She knew she was a successful manager, but like a true 10xer, she believed that if she knew herself better, she could drive greater results for her team and her company and make sure the best members got the advancement they deserved.

"By putting the oxygen mask on myself, I got enough space to ask important questions. Did I myself have room for growth? Could I be happy here in the long run? Was I growing? Was my boss continuing to give me the feedback and opportunities I really needed to grow? And most of all, did I still feel satisfied? At the end of the day, there's no point in just blaming your boss. I figure, if my boss is not the one who can help me tackle my problems, I have to be able to turn to someone for managerial guidance. It's my responsibility."

Sure enough, by having the courage to switch hats and address her own issues as a talent, Cathy gained some meaningful insight into ways she could help her team move forward. Certain blind spots made themselves apparent, and she found ways to help herself that motivated those around her. She knew what to ask of her boss, and, in turn, her own reports were the better for it.

On Cathy's team was a star developer named Doug—a talent in every sense of the word. He also benefited from sessions with the company's coach. Doug had spent his whole year being a good soldier, delivering on the mandates Cathy and the company handed him, but he too felt the need to stop the wheel and switch hats. For Doug, that meant thinking like a manager.

"I knew I was doing my part as a coder," Doug explains, "but, to be honest, I hadn't really taken the time to evaluate those around me and see if I was helping to meet their needs....it just didn't feel right."

First and foremost, Doug had to ask if he was giving Cathy the tools she needed to be able to properly evaluate him. He also had to explore which peers on his team could most benefit from his help. He, too, started asking tough questions: Have I watched out for the others on my team? Have I done anything to help elevate my worthiest peers? "I started asking around, seeing what people would most like or need from me, to help them optimize. I wasn't 'playing manager' exactly, but I was trying to see how I could be of maximum service and provide guidance when it was needed. I mean, if we can't help each other, what's the point?"

As with Cathy, Doug's plan didn't work perfectly, and some met his inquiries with puzzled looks and nothing constructive to add, but the ones who got it were able to truly help him advance his skills and tackle his deficiencies.

Just as Cathy's hat-switch energized those around her, Doug's brought him closer to many colleagues and fortified team spirit. Not everyone had immediate answers or requests for him, but everyone deeply appreciated the common sense way he went about offering his time and attention.

When in doubt, switch hats. You may learn some surprising things about the way forward.

Leadership and learning are indispensable to each other.
—JOHN F. KENNEDY, 1963

HOW WE ROLL

In the process of writing this chapter, we couldn't help but note to ourselves just how often we are called upon in our daily work to switch hats. It's definitely not something we were comfortable with at first—we always saw ourselves as managers in a very traditional sense, and we were damn proud of it. But after decades behind the scenes, managing and advising a wide array of different talents, we started 10x Management. This meant becoming "the face of a brand," building a business in a totally new sector with a totally new concept, and we knew we were out of our element. There was just no getting around the fact that we needed guidance. That's when we turned to Jonathan Lowenhar of the consulting firm Enjoy The Work, whom you met in Chapter 3.

Today, we have elected to have Lowenhar be our advisor (think: manager), to help us in all of the ways that we describe in this book. When we're in his presence, he wears the manager hat and we become the talent.

We speak every week, meet quarterly, and stage events with him twice a year. He helps us create big picture long-term strategic goals, and works with us to plan shorter term tactics and priorities to help us reach those goals. He works hard to get alignment between us when there's a fissure, and always delivers honest feedback about our weaknesses and blind spots. He also brings much-needed functional expertise in those areas of the business where we have room to improve; in our case, sales and marketing expertise, along with sales tracking and data collection.

One of Lowenhar's most important roles is challenging our limiting beliefs about growth and possibilities. However, he's no mollycoddler. His most recurring question is, "If you want X, are you willing to do Y?"

By allowing ourselves to switch hats, Lowenhar has helped us understand what we are good at and what we need help with. This has proven especially effective when we need to focus our efforts in the moment. Like many entrepreneurs, we can get easily distracted and lose the plot. It doesn't help much that we're managers. Only another manager can get us back on track when we've lost our way.

One of the reasons we cherish Lowenhar's advice so much is because he instinctively understands the Double-Hat balance. He recently told us about a new founder he's been working with. "She is of exceptional skill," he said. "I'm convinced she could shut down her current company, start a new venture, and in mere days raise capital for whatever she might dream of next. But . . . for me to support her fully really requires two separate lenses. The first lens is to see her as Talent. Is she realizing her own potential? Are there skills that would expand her impact or get her closer to her goals? The second lens is to see her as Manager of her own career. She has infinite career choice. What is the opportunity cost of her current endeavor? What other options might be nurtured? While she's entrusted my firm with advancing her skills as a unique talent, it's primarily her responsibility to manage her career choices, to live the life she truly wants."

Not surprisingly, Lowenhar himself gets managed when it's required or desired. As the sole owner of his company Enjoy The Work, he doesn't have built-in management or supervision, so, in true 10x fashion, he elected to create a board of directors to play that managerial role for him. He had only one motivation to do this: He knew that outside POV would help him and benefit his company.

And so it's almost like Russian dolls: We are full-time managers with a manager, and that manager has managers of his own who likely have managers of their own, too.

Once you've committed to wearing both hats at the right time, you are ready for maximum growth, maximum understanding.

In our final chapter, we'll take those two hats to the negotiation table— and explore how to get the most from any deal.

THE DOUBLE-HAT CONTINUUM

The 0xer	Believes they are either manager or talent, but doesn't realize that, in order to live the life they want and have the career they want, they need to be both.
The 5xer	Knows that they need to be both manager and talent, but rarely remembers to pick their heads up out of the weeds, and pay attention to what role is presently needed most.
The 10xer	Switches hats with finesse, frequently and as needed, in order to achieve their own goals and tend to their flock, all while never losing sight of the big picture.

TAKEAWAYS FROM CHAPTER 9

- Today, we are living in a Double-Hat World, where everyone must learn to be adept at both the talent and the management role.
- This means managers must reframe themselves as talent some of the time, in order to help contextualize their career.
- For talent, this means being able to provide great management to the many people whose careers you have a stake in, and who affect your career.
- Switching hats isn't always easy and doesn't always feel natural, but talent has to learn how to lead, and managers have to learn how to treat themselves as solo practitioners.
- The 10xer donning two hats is capable of both absorbing useful feedback even when it's negative and delivering the right amount of praise to others.
- Rapid changes in the marketplace mean greater instability and the need for more agility. Being able to wear two hats makes you twice as valuable.
- "Rising tides raise all boats," and managers who can act as talent as well as talent who can act as management create a positive atmosphere where maximum growth is possible.

1 2 3 4 5 6 7 8 9 **10**

THE EVOLUTION OF THE DEAL

Talent hits a target no one else can hit.
Genius hits a target no one else can see.
—ARTHUR SCHOPENHAUER, 1844

BOTH SIDES OF THE TABLE

We've spent the last nine chapters making the case for how the world of work has changed, what companies need to do to adjust to that change, and what individuals can do to strive for 10xness in this new world order. We also aimed to make the case that donning two hats is not only possible but imperative.

Now we're going to shift gears again, and close on a much more tactical topic: What changes do companies need to make in order to actually land 10x-level talent?

It's a timely question, because the old procurement processes don't really address the way the new world works and companies and governments need to make major changes to their approach or risk ceding competitive advantage to those that do.

Nowhere is the facility for donning two hats more valuable than when approaching the negotiation table. In the old school mode, employer and employee (or potential employee) in negotiation were like defense and prosecution, hellbent on "protecting their own interests." According to an etymological study conducted by the *Journal of Business Communication*,[1] the term "win-win" didn't even begin to appear until the 1970s, when it first showed up in academic papers on conflict management. By the early '80s, "win-win" was all over the trade press, but it was definitely not yet standard practice for HR personnel. In all but the rarest of cases, employers usually had the lion's share of power, and therefore they defined the parameters of what constituted a successful contract.

That market, with its rock-steady imbalance, is no more.

In fact, even the ancient math of salary-plus-hours-equals-job is a relic. Today, for all the most important roles, every employment contract negotiation (whether for a W2 or a 1099) must be treated as a dance toward a multifaceted pact, shaped to custom-fit the needs of both the worker and the company. What we can't emphasize enough is that 10xers are each unique, with widely varying backgrounds, a unique set of career goals and objectives, and a singular viewpoint about how they want to make their contribution to the overall landscape.

What amazes us more than anything is that some big companies who are smart in so many other ways still haven't gotten this memo. The deal-making evolution is well underway, yet a majority of larger corporations insist on trying to entice their favored candidates with cookie cutter offers. Furthermore, it shocks them when they aren't able to catch the best and the brightest.

Differing views on negotiation are at the heart of this disconnect.

For better or worse, our society values dealmaking as much as it values anything. The signed contract is as American as "hot dogs, apple pie, and Chevrolet." Top lawyers, agents, advisors are usually the fierce players who represent those at the top—athletes, entertainers, CEOs, entrepreneurs. There are dozens of books out there on the art of the deal, and whether or not you like them or their authors, you can't deny that they often find their way to the top of the New York Times Best Seller list.

The deal is its own kind of star, and at the end of the day, all business is essentially a series of deals.

But what does dealmaking in the new world really consist of? Just what *is* on the table during a contemporary negotiation with a 10xer? Under the right circumstances—everything. But you have to be able to read each situation. In our view, it starts with understanding the wants and needs of the candidate. Then it moves to the big questions: Who has the strongest leverage? How can each side create or fortify their own leverage? What unseen parameters does this agreement fail to address? And, once signed, how will this pact play out in the long run?

It's more open than you think.

BESPOKE NEGOTIATION

For the talent, and its manager (and that could mean an employment attorney, a sage friend, or an agent), negotiation is about understanding the talent's true desires and presenting them in a reasonable and considerate manner, with one eye on the hiring company's needs. Gathering all that data takes work.

In Chapter 2, we introduced you to our Lifestyle Calculator (https://10xascend.com/calculator/), the tool we use to help our 10x Ascend clients evaluate their preferences before an important employment negotiation. As we mentioned, the Calculator explores twenty-four attributes, and the results are *never* the same. No two talents are ever looking for the exact same work scenario. One CEO we spoke with likes to begin his process by asking candidates the following question.

If you had to choose one, which would it be:

1. *Work/life balance?*

2. *Meaningful work?*
3. *Great compensation?*

He knows that just by getting that one answer, he has some insight into who he's dealing with. We go a bit deeper but certainly applaud the thinking of beginning with a question which can help you understand the candidate. Having empathy and seeing the other side of the table will lead you to more closed deals than any other factor.

By applying the results of twenty-four elements of the Lifestyle Calculator to the inner workings of the hiring process, we have learned that we can often create an *alignment context* that is every bit as important as the basics of the deal. In other words, you never know for sure just what's going to get you to that win-win—it may not be the most obvious bargaining chip. Though it's true that leverage can come from having a "stalking horse," i.e. a competing offer, in fact, there are a multitude of ways for companies and prospects to create leverage. In some instances, what leads to a breakthrough is less about leverage and more about clearly explaining and justifying why a given candidate wants some specific element or elements of an offer to change.

At the opening of this book, we told you about Jake, the brilliant coder who was passed over by a midsized pharma outfit, mostly because they couldn't fathom his desire to work remotely. We were better able to help the education tech firm, who could picture Jake getting the work done right, even if they wouldn't get to watch it unfold in real-time. With a receptive party, leverage can come in all shapes and sizes.

To give you some additional context, here are a few case studies from our negotiation experiences. When viewed back to back, they demonstrate that a wide variety of elements can be at stake when you arrive at the negotiation table. They also clearly demonstrate that when you have the right in-demand skill sets, and the right approach, great strides can be achieved. These are all real clients, but because compensation is a private matter, we've obscured some identifying features. Still, the stories are not only true, they're par for the course.

Case Number One: Finding the Key Line Item

In Q1 of a busy recent year, a senior technologist came to us with early stage offers from both Google and Salesforce. In his 30 year career, he'd never really negotiated any of his prior job offers. This time, however, he wanted to do everything in his power to make sure his next move was a strong one, so he engaged us. Changing jobs meant leaving a secure position at Microsoft where he'd been working happily for years. He was in excellent standing there, with room for growth. Still, his gut told him it was time for a change.

Our approach was straightforward. We had him explore the twenty-four elements using our Lifestyle Calculator and determined that *paid time off* was going to be a huge factor in whatever his next move would be. On the cusp of earning five weeks of vacation every year at Microsoft, he didn't want to make a move and get less—in fact, he wanted greater flexibility involving when, and how often he could take time off. It might seem like a negligible line item, an afterthought, but knowing a single, key piece of information like this can change everything when it's time to come to terms.

We also discovered, by evaluating the two initial offers, that there was room for improvement with some of the more typical items, like salary, equity compensation, and bonuses. We helped him craft a multistage negotiation strategy and provided on-the-fly advice throughout. Together we developed a series of counteroffers that left nothing off the table. We also provided talking points and composed emails for him to send to his prospective employers. Every now and then he would refer to his advisor's insights and market data in these emails, which lent credibility to his asks and eliminated negotiation friction. Because he could refer to "his advisor's data," he essentially employed the Third Party Effect.

Naturally, with two competing offers, we leveraged them against each other. Where one was low in equity, the other was low in bonuses and paid time off—his key want. Sharing select information with each company regarding "the other offer" allowed us to improve both deals and give him a better choice. Ultimately, we were able to increase the base salary of one of the offers by 35 percent and increase the equity of the other offer by an equivalent amount.

We're happy to report that, working together, we ultimately scored him a total compensation package that was exponentially improved, but that wasn't the only big win. Crucially, the winning company was able to give this talent what he wanted *most*: the right amount of flexible vacation time. He was now able to choose based on which company felt like a better fit, rather than who offered the better initial package. Given that he would spend most of his waking hours serving this company, choosing the right one—the one he'd feel better at—was as important as the compensation.

Because they were smart, forward-thinking companies, they received all our requests and explanations not as threats and demands, but rather as insights that were important to a talent that they knew would make a real impact for their company. They also were able to be creative enough within their respective bureaucracies to get things approved that would never have flown at many large companies.

Case Number Two: The Power of Benchmarking

We met with two senior cyber security technologists who were being re-cruited together by HSBC to build teams with their highly specialized expertise. Obviously, this is a major international financial institution with tens of thousands of dedicated employees, but these two guys were also nothing to mess with. One was working with DARPA, the other had done a stint with the FBI. The new opportunity, as interesting as it sounded, meant that both candidates would need to relocate from the US to the UK. After months of going back and forth on their own, the bank still hadn't made an offer. By the time they got to us, the two candidates were tired of the strain of the slow-moving process and ready for guidance and closure, even if that closure meant that the offers were dead. They knew this opportunity could be huge for them, despite the fact that it meant losing the seemingly unheard-of job security and comfort their gigs with the federal government offered.

With this in mind, our first priority was to provide the candidates with messaging designed to prompt the bank to make a concrete offer. Within two weeks, the bank delivered, but initial terms were generic and under-whelming, though we believed the bank *thought* they were putting their best foot forward. As we often encounter, their first offer was based on the bank's evaluation of market value mixed with their internal compensation bands, rather than the candidates' true worth on the open market. The data that companies use when evaluating what to put in an offer is prob-lematic, usually derived from sources which don't factor in 10xers. Their "facts," based on averages, are also indicative of the significant majority of workers who don't negotiate. These data points, skewed in favor of em-ployers, don't speak for 10xers, and 10xers don't take them seriously.

The bank's initial offer wasn't merely weak. It also failed to address many of the candidates' stated relocation concerns and all the risk in-volved in leaving their very secure cushy jobs along with moving their fam-ilies across the world. It was a non-starter.

We knew it was on us to unearth and justify the offer's missing com-ponents as well as resetting the conversation to a different playing field. One of the biggest misalignments was around relocation. The move from the US to the UK would be a significant sacrifice and disruption for both candidates and their families. Moreover, making this kind of move car-ried greater risk because it meant leaving secure jobs. A "normal" offer (salary, vacation, title, bonus, and so forth) was simply not going to cut the mustard.

We developed a counterproposal that included relocation allowance, relocation trips to the new city for each candidate and their families, school search assistance and education consultancy for each of their de-pendents, an educational consultant to help them find the right schools, support for private school with consideration of the differences between

US and European school systems, temporary housing support, and tax education and adjustments.

Writing up and delivering this counterproposal was just the beginning of the process. We then worked closely with the candidates to develop and deploy a multistage negotiating strategy that included pivots and iterations as the bank responded and as new data emerged. Though we don't have some secret magic source for pulling data together, we do have 50 years of combined negotiation experience and some best practices we rely on. The key is knowing what case you need to make for each situation. Then, you go out and find the supporting data. We use the information we have, such as how much a client is already making, our own database of past deals, as well as general internet sleuthing. Our biggest tricks here are looking everywhere and anywhere for data, always keeping in mind that most random compensation information out there in the world is skewed by the fact that more than 60 percent of people don't negotiate their job offers at all. With that in mind, you need to know that the numbers for those who do are higher than those averages you see posted on the popular compensation sites.

Over the course of this negotiation, we served in both an advisory and hands-on negotiating role. Initially we ghost-wrote emails and provided talking points for the candidates to present to the bank. Later, the candidates asked us to step in and directly negotiate on their behalf with HR.

Three weeks after we got involved, both candidates had secured offers that they were excited about. Naturally, we were happy about that, but the real moral of the story is that we couldn't have gotten them there without educating both sides. Our benchmarking gave the candidates data that helped them to not only demonstrate their own worth, but also sent a clear message about what it would take to build the teams they were hired to create. Deep data showed that the bank's current salary ranges were just not competitive. Best of all, sharing this info prompted a departmental reassessment that even led to a significant increase for their manager-to-be, who had been undervalued based on our metrics.

You know you're starting on the good foot when your negotiations also result in your new supervisor getting a raise!

Again, it's important to note that none of these successes ever happen if the company in question doesn't understand the value that a given talent (and similar talents) will bring to their organization. Only after realizing how much they needed to adjust, in order to land the talent that they wanted, were they willing to address the various negotiation items. Attracting 10x talent simply *requires* a different, more bespoke strategy!

Looking back, our success was not only driven by the bank's desire to hire these guys. The real linchpin came when we explained that they would never be able to hire the complete team that was needed to execute their plans if they didn't rethink their strategy. Our guys were clear: *If you give us what we want, but then go back to where you've been, it will all be for naught, as we won't be able to do what you're hiring us for.*

Case Number Three: The Bird in Hand

We were approached by a senior DevOps engineer who was being courted by Facebook and another large publicly traded technology company. The offers intrigued her, but she was very happily employed at Salesforce. From us, she wanted help navigating her options.

Our first questions formed the basis of our approach:

1. *What mattered most for her life and lifestyle?*

As with most of our clients, completing the Lifestyle Calculator prompted her to think about the hiring process in a completely different manner. What started as a few points to improve (salary and equity) became a much more robust and colorful composite, including paid time off, flexibility on time in office, and a budget for conferences and continuing professional development and education.

2. *What was reasonable compensation for someone with her experience and knowledge?*

We evaluated her offers not only against her current compensation, but also against comparable offers to others at her level, making adjustments to those numbers for the reasons stated in the previous section. We discovered that there was a lot of room for improvement with salary, equity compensation, and bonuses.

By exploring what was most important to her, we had uncovered two key points of leverage. First, she had competing suitors that we could play off of each other. Second, she was very content and secure in her current position. To move, there had to be an upside, a significant one. Having a job you love is rare. Working that job somewhere you also love is rarer. You don't jump ship for nothing.

With this in mind, the first thing we did was slow down negotiations with the company that was farther along in the process while speeding up negotiations with the other. We let both suitors know that they were going to need to make compelling and competitive offers if they really wanted to catch this talent. One of the companies came in with a very aggressive offer; the other made an anemic bid that was lower by every metric.

Still, we were only getting started.

The second step was to craft a "dream counteroffer" that factored in *everything* that was important to the client, including a great salary, a strong equity package, more paid time off, and a budget for continuing education and conferences. It was a stretch, but a justified one. Worst case scenario, she would keep the job she loved.

The third step of our strategy was to focus on improving the better of the two initial offers, because their enthusiasm indicated greater potential. She had a greater interest in the work they were offering, in part because they had taken the time, during the interview process, to explain to her why they wanted *her* and not just anyone for this job. They showed her that they thought she was uniquely suited to help them achieve a very important set of goals for the company. We approached them with a carefully constructed counteroffer and told them that, if they met all of our requests by a certain date, we would not seek a counteroffer from Facebook.

They bit, and their new offer met nearly every one of our requests. Our client felt it was close enough to her dream package to justify the move. We more than doubled her compensation, nabbed her a title bump, and got her more paid vacation as well as the right budget for education and conferences. Finally, we helped ensure a smooth transition by clarifying her reporting structure.

Once again, we had to zero in on what she really wanted—*and* educate the prospective company about why those wants were legit—to make the "win-win" manifest.

It's important to note that all of the prior cases were negotiations for full-time W2 employees. In fact, the W2 itself is a bargaining chip, and not every 10xer wants a corporate lockdown.

When negotiating for freelancers, which we do daily at 10x Management, it usually goes like this:

We say, "X person is $300/hour."

The customer says, "Wow, that is really expensive."

We kindly explain that they don't yet have the missing variable to determine that. We go on to explain that they need to compare what each person can deliver at the end of an hour. If someone is $150/hour and produces a solution in 10 hours, you spent $1,500 on the "cheaper" resource, but if the same work is complete by the $300/hour person in 3 hours, you've saved $600. Without the big picture, you can't make sane decisions.

In the final analysis, the best companies rarely balk at any request, no matter how far-flung. They listen, learn, and do the smart thing, the thing that will actually benefit them in the end. At root, the best companies understand that talent calls the shots. After all, what is the workplace without talent?

L.E.A.P. BEFORE YOU LOOK

So far, we've focused on what companies need to do to be more competitive in their hiring practices. Despite our dream that one day all companies will adopt these ideas, the fact is that many will not, which is why we also need to arm talent with the tactics they need so they can help companies come around to a more evolved way of thinking.

When talking about employment, you often hear people say things like "It's a two-way street," Or, "You're interviewing the company just as much as they're interviewing you." Nice sentiments, but despite this basic logic, consider the list of things an employer almost always controls (or at least tries to):

- Job descriptions and expectations
- Required experience level
- When and where interviews take place
- Who sits in on the interview
- Timeline for next steps

To combat this radical imbalance, we've created an Employment *List of Expectations and Priorities*, aka an Employment L.E.A.P.—a document written by a job candidate and presented to an employer to help them understand what that candidate hopes to get out of an employment agreement.

Our hypothesis here is simple: If the company can provide a detailed document about what they want, aka a job description, why shouldn't the candidate do the same?

To be clear, an Employment L.E.A.P. isn't a job description or a resume per se, but there can be some overlap with both. An Employment L.E.A.P. should take the dialogue a step further, and explain a talent's true expectations, priorities, and goals for what they hope to get out of being an employee for a particular company, including salary and many of the other attributes from the Lifestyle Calculator, desires for company culture, and *any* details regarding a potential work arrangement.

Through an Employment L.E.A.P., a talent can reclaim some of the power in the exchange by putting their own expectations on the table. Yes, the company is looking for the perfect candidate fit, but *you're* looking for the perfect company—it's a marriage with equal vows.

Of course, it's important not to jump the gun and present an Employment L.E.A.P. too early. A talent will only want to submit this document after convincing the company of their basic value, once it looks like things might actually be moving forward and the company has signaled they are likely to make an offer. The other obvious time to lay it on the line is when they ask about your salary requirements. This document should be very helpful for the employer as well, since they now know more about what kind of offer will move the needle for this candidate.

So what does an Employment L.E.A.P. actually look like?

The L.E.A.P. itself—*and* the framing of it—must be tailored to the situation. But for those looking to draw inspiration, here's a rough template.

The L.E.A.P. Email

Dear > *First Name of Hiring Party*, <

Thanks so much for all the time thus far. As it would seem we are moving into the phase where we discuss the parameters of a deal and my employment, I took the liberty of creating a Employment List of Expectations and Priorities. This is a new-ish concept used to help companies make offers that best meet the goals of both the employee and the employer.

A few very important notes: I am hopeful this document will be helpful in understanding what is important to me and will not in any way be perceived as presumptuous. I fully recognize that some of my hopes may not be possible in the confines of your policies and precedent, but I would be remiss if I was not clear in what my priorities are.

I don't expect to get everything on this list, but do want to have an open and honest dialogue. I know that when empowered with this information, companies get more deals done and achieve better employee/employer satisfaction and retention.

In short, I am saying that there is value for both of us in this document. After you have had a chance to review, please let me know if you have questions. If it is all clear, I very much look forward to receiving your offer and working toward becoming a part of your team.

The L.E.A.P. Doc

Dear > *First Name of Hiring Party*, <

I am submitting this Employment List of Expectations and Priorities in an effort to explain my expectations for the > Name of Role < at > Name of Company <. It is my hope that this will help > Name of Company < craft an offer that allows us to swiftly move forward and begin working together soon.

For this role, I am seeking the following:

- Base Salary: x-y (X should equal the lowest you would accept for this job if everything else relating to the offer was exactly as you would want it and Y should be the highest that you could imagine them or a similar company paying for this role if everything else about the offer was terrible.)
- Bonus: x
- Equity: $x vesting over y years
- Vacation (Paid Time Off): x days/year
- Starting Title: > Title <
- Flex Time: The ability to work from home or remotely x days / week or month
- Pension, Health & Other Benefits: > Questions or Concerns <

- Relocation budget (If applicable): What is your policy on this? I have heard you often provide funding for the move and housing for the first 6 months.
- Office: I have a strong preference for an office with a door as I do my most productive and best work without too many distractions.
- Outside Projects: This would be where you list any board seats or outside projects you hope to continue while under their employment.
- Anything else on your wish list:

Thank you for taking the time to consider my goals for this role. I sincerely hope they will be helpful. I'm excited by the possibility of moving forward with > Name of Company <.

Best regards, > Name <

Obviously, these are ballpark setups, but what's most important is that every talent find a way to balance out the employer-employee power dynamic by clearly communicating expectations for their potential role. If you can pass this info along through a manager or a credible Third Party, even better. When executed properly, this simple act of self-disclosure can minimize the number of negotiation cycles, bring to fruition a much healthier starting point, and head off a wide variety of future conflicts.

DO YOU BELIEVE IN MAGIC?

When music biz game changer James Diener (Maroon 5, Avril Lavigne, Gavin DeGraw, et al.) steps into a negotiation, he deploys techniques they don't teach in business school. And not just any techniques. We're talking magic techniques. A longstanding member of the Academy of Magical Arts, Diener has been performing card magic for as long as he can remember.

"I haven't really left home without a deck of cards since I was about ten or eleven," he told us. "It's one of the biggest passions of my life, and it actually dovetails with my perspective on business."

However, it's not like Diener does hocus pocus and hypnotizes the people he's negotiating with! It's more like magic studies have primed him for the vicissitudes of contract negotiation. "Among the benefits of studying magic," Diener explains, "is the fact that you have to put in *a lot a lot a lot* of effort to get even basic results."

Diener says that, like a martial art or an academic discipline, it takes years to be able to create the necessary mystery and illusion to pull off just a few effects properly. "Through magic, I learned discipline and patience," he says. "And even more important, effects that I learned ten or fifteen years ago, I still optimize, iterate, tweak—you're constantly learning. Just like the business world, if you aren't willing to work hard enough and invest in the preparatory work, you're going to be headed for a difficult time."

When we asked Diener if that meant he brought a "poker face" to the negotiation table he quickly corrected us. "Not at all," he said. "It's the reverse in magic. Connecting is everything. Let's say you and I were each going to learn a card effect. Okay, we'd both master the method, there'd probably be some sleight of hand involved, and in theory, we would be able to perform the same effect with the same ability and get the same reaction from an audience, right? Now, in order to take it to the next level, a magician striving to be great will have to learn what is called *spectator management*."

Diener describes this magnificent term as the ability to refine and adjust the performance of a magic effect based on who's watching, how many people are watching, what portions of the audience are watching, where they're seated, what genders are present, where you're standing in relation to whom, and more. Every nuance counts.

"Are you standing in front of a group of females or are there couples to your right? Are you performing for a bunch of guys at the bar? Are they drinking? Is the environment quiet, loud? You're constantly reading the room and *adjusting the way the effect rolls out.*

The difference between a "skilled" magician and a 10x magician, as Diener explains it, is the ability to *manage the momentum* of the effect in relation to the spectators' responses, all in real time. "That's the difference," Diener says, "the secret to creating an extraordinary and awesome outcome in magic, and the same goes for creating a successful deal. People who perhaps came from a strict law school or business school and have read every textbook there is, may still not have had the practical, interpersonal experience it takes to really understand spectator management. You use it as you're catching your deals, moving them forward, with every interaction, every email, every conference call."

Diener says a real magician loves to perform anywhere and everywhere, but sometimes it's about knowing when *not* to perform. "A good magician can walk into a room and know, 'This is not going to be a positive interaction.' Because they work to understand—what's the mood of the people around? Are they looking to be interrupted and entertained? Maybe they don't want interference right now? Or maybe there's conflict in the room? You want to find those opportunities where 85 percent has been *de-risked* before you even produce a deck of cards."

In contract negotiation and in magic, rookies plow ahead. They will, as Diener puts it, *presume* that people are ready and excited and open, and fail because of that one act of presumption. Timing is key, and Diener will sometimes wait to the last minute to present an effect or pitch his ideas, so that the sense of anticipation and open ears has grown acute.

"How many times have I been sitting there in a meeting where I know somebody is going to pitch something or try to get an idea in, but the room is just not ready for it. Or worse, people are already demonstrating resistance to other issues, so they aren't going to be open to what you're pitching next. I try to stay attentive to this type of stuff. If you're thinking about it, you have a better chance of succeeding than if you're not thinking about it."

To illustrate spectator management, Diener told us a great story about a high-pressure moment with a platinum musical act who shall remain nameless. At the time, as Diener explains it, this musical act was newly on the rise and the record company was excited about an upcoming important promotional phase for the project.

Getting the international and national arm of a major record company to put the resources behind a developing artist is no small accomplishment, one that most musical acts would kill for. This is something only bestowed on the priority performers who typically represent less than 5 percent of the records being released at a given time. However, upon hearing the news, Diener's act hesitated. They wanted to make creative changes and revisions to album repertoire, previously approved, before being inclined to proceed, even though their record company was excited to move forward immediately and pursuant to a tightly scheduled game plan.

One of the members of this musical act, in particular, was campaigning for lengthy new recording revisions.

"*Re-record* is one of the worst words in the English language," Diener says with a laugh.

The clock was ticking, and a video had already been shot for several hundred thousand dollars. The band's management turned to Diener and said, "I can't convince them that re-recording is a mistake. Maybe you can."

"I tried talking to the artist on the phone," Diener says, "but conference calls with musicians are extremely difficult and disadvantageous. You need the eye contact to assess and resolve issues productively. And the only way to have a meeting with them was to travel out of state, unscheduled at last minute, to a local concert and hold a direct meeting. So that's what the core label creative team did. Sitting backstage, the parties got down to negotiation—release the current version or re-record? The first part of the conversation was rational, getting the facts out on the table. The record company was prepared to risk huge sums to give this version the shot they felt it deserved. Still, the more the band was confronted with logic, the more defiant they became, and the more entrenched. Technically, the record label had the power to override them and authorize the release of the current music previously approved, but Diener felt that it would not be prudent to override recording artists and risk their creative trust for an act he cherished by doing something irreversible. "Musicians don't like to be coerced. Telling them, *'Here's how it is and you'll just have to live with it'* would have haunted us for years to come."

Stuck as he was, Diener's only recourse was to work his spectator management magic. He watched the discussion. He observed.

"I noticed a schism between two of the members," he recalls. "It was subtle, but it was there—they might have acted like they were on the same page but they weren't."

From that little piece of hidden data, Diener began to wonder if there weren't more opinions in the room than were being openly expressed. Taking a chance, he called for a blind vote. He even offered to leave so they could discuss it among themselves, and then he passed out napkins for the final anonymous tally.

Strangely enough, there was a majority consensus to put the music out as-is. A strong spectator reading, followed by a little bit of theatrics and a bold risk move, uncovered the truth and restored harmony for all involved.

One of the reasons Diener is so astute at reading the "spectators" involved in music biz negotiation is that he himself has played so many roles—as label head, record producer, A&R exec, manager, and more. The ability to switch hats has particularly helped him with dealmaking, even during disagreements with the counterparty, because he's been in their shoes and always makes a conscious effort to exercise empathy.

What may be surprising to some is that empathy in negotiation pays dividends.

Diener says, "People who are taught, formally or informally, that the way to do business is to extract every possible concession you can get from the other side can only see the transaction uniquely, as opposed to one in a constellation of many transactions. I operate from the belief that the only thing that *really* matters is how people feel leaving the transaction. Wrong or right, I assume that this will be one of many times I will ultimately interact with this counterparty. So if they remember the positive experience, it's worth more than what we could get if I grind them down for more."

Sometimes, Diener will round up in the other party's favor to show that his main concern is not the decimal points. Unsurprisingly, it makes future deals easier and quicker to close. Diener also believes that counterparties can usually sense when a request is "need-based" rather than "desire-based" and it creates for a tenser, less successful negotiation.

"If you don't operate from a place of empathy," Diener says, "you're always at the mercy of each individual transaction. You've got no *reputational currency* that you're accumulating, which you can use later, like a wild card to throw in when you're working on a more difficult situation."

Reputational currency—it works like magic.

The Manager Test

Just as the manager needs to evaluate the talent, the talent must also be vetting for the team they will be joining. There is nothing worse than getting to your new role only to discover you've made a horrible mistake. Here are a few basic questions to ask yourself *before* you ink that contract:

1. How much did they ask about you, your interests, and your goals? Did they show any concern for you, or were they only interested in how you can benefit them?
2. Did they ask you anything about how you have grown from previous experiences? Great managers are looking for people in a state of constant evolution. The best know how to tease this out of a candidate with carefully constructed questions that cover the arc and growth of someone's career. If they didn't pan for that gold, they may not be the right managers for you.

3. During your interview, did you give yourself an opportunity to disagree about something minor? You can back off of this kind of disagreement very quickly but in the process, you may learn a ton about the person sitting across the table with this trick (special thanks Jonathan Lowenhar for sharing it). If they instantly feel threatened or get their hackles up, you now know that working with them will likely be "their way or the highway." If you are okay with that, so be it, but make it a choice. It is important to note that if you execute this trick poorly, you might blow your opportunity, so tread lightly after having carefully read the room (see Do You Believe in Magic? earlier in this chapter).

4. Did you ask your interviewers probing questions about the company culture? Did you bring up any of the following? What hours do people work? Do they work remotely? Do people take vacation? Are they expected to be on call while on vacation? What are the company's values if they exist at all? Are those values on record? What does the interviewer love about working for this company? What is the best thing about this team of people? What is the worst?

In the one life you have been given, you may be spending between 40-60 hours per week with these people and this company, working on their projects and absorbing their atmosphere. Make sure you know what you are getting into with reasonable but granular clarity.

DELIVERING THE QUAN

In 1996's wildly popular movie *Jerry Maguire,* about a sports agent on the skids, Jerry (played by Tom Cruise) asks his client, football player Rod Tidwell (played by Cuba Gooding Jr.) what he's really after. Tidwell's answer is one of cinema's most memorable invented words—*the quan*. But what is it?

"Love, respect, community, and the dollars, too, the entire package," Tidwell explains, shutting his eyes and making a rainbow with his open hands. *"The quan."*

What's brilliant about this made-up concept is the way it amalgamates several forces that don't necessarily go hand in hand. However, as Tidwell is suggesting, only the right talent and the right management working in tandem can make it happen.

In order to illustrate how all aspects of the talent-management axis can work together to deliver "the quan," we think it will be helpful to give you an overview of the career arc of one of our clients. Think of it as the basic ideas of this book, played out in one brief period of just one career.

Although we changed the name of the client as well as the names of the companies mentioned, the basic scenarios outlined here are more than real—they represent an arc we've seen with many 10xers.

When we first started working with Elliot, we knew three things, two that were obvious up front: first, that he had an exceptional mind especially given his young age; second, that he had not been getting valued in a manner commensurate with his abilities. The third thing that impressed us, which we gleaned over time, was that Elliot possessed a powerful *success impulse*. He asked the right questions. He was interested in hearing feedback right away. And he was hungry to learn, even though he already knew so much.

As with most of our client relationships, the first thing we did was work with Elliot to get a better understanding of what his *bespoke career goals* were. What types of projects excited him? Which of his skill sets did he prefer to use over others? We wanted to get a general sense of how he wanted to use his knowledge to help others while still enjoying the process.

Since the structure of our relationship with our client is such that we don't earn anything if they don't earn anything, Elliot quickly understood that the value proposition of our work could only be win-win. We had *skin in the game*—his success would be our success and vice versa.

At the time, we were working very hard to establish our boutique agency as the go-to resource for companies to gain rapid access to the best and the brightest tech freelancers. Elliot observed our efforts and knew that the more effective we were at building our brand, the better the offers would be from participating companies—offers that he himself could take advantage of. From our vantage point, we knew that the more sophisticated our talent was, the more effective we could be in helping those companies find the right resources to solve their thorniest tech problems. This synergy of viewpoints enhanced the *sense of mutual trust* that was developing between Elliot and ourselves.

We put Elliot on a variety of gigs, where he demonstrated that he was incredibly capable and fast (as in *superhuman fast*), leaving a trail of very happy and often astounded customers in his wake. The win-win was in full effect.

Around this time, a company came to us looking for crypto talent, a perfect fit for Elliot as he himself was a very early adapter to bitcoin and cryptocurrency in general. We scored the gig for Elliot, garnering him his highest rate ever, in large part because we were able to accurately boast about how good and fast his work was. *The Third Party Effect* strikes again.

At the outset, the crypto engagement was solidified as a fairly straightforward contract engagement. Elliot was going to create a very significant never-before-built crypto exchange for them, and he would remain a freelancer while doing so, able to take on projects with other companies if he desired. We helped ensure that Elliot was compensated properly for his time and that the terms of the agreement were fair, equitable, and crystal clear. The engagement went off without a hitch and Elliot was thrilled to make as much as he did. Ultimately, the company was so happy with Elliot's work that they came to us asking if he would be willing to consider an offer to join their team full time, as a W2 employee. At the time, Elliot wasn't really looking for a full-time position, but he had enjoyed working on the project and was excited about what the company was building. In short, he was willing to consider an offer.

Before taking the leap, however, we worked with Elliot to get him to really think about what was important to him in a full-time position. We had not yet developed our formal Lifestyle Calculator, but this was part of the impetus for its creation. Once the questioning process was complete, we helped Elliot negotiate the full-time offer. We helped him get the salary he was hoping for, the equity he desired, and a title that we felt was in line with his level of skill. We also ensured he was able to work remotely from halfway across the country which was very important to him. This meant that he had no state income tax, allowing a greater portion of his impressive salary to stay in his hands. Once again, the Third Party Effect was instrumental in making Elliot's case for him.

It's important to note that, at the time, Elliot himself didn't much care about title, but we felt it was important, because it would be the launchpad for future titles and offers should he elect to remain in the W2 corporate world when this job had run its course. These insights were our way of sharing *Super Vision*—future forecasting in action.

Fast forward a few years. Elliot loved working at the company, he'd made a substantial impact on their product offering, but now he was itching for other challenges. He opted to leave the company and start freelancing again, and he wanted our help finding the right engagements. Thus, a similar cycle started anew.

Elliot went on to work freelance on another crypto project, and, once again, the company was so blown away that they wanted to hire him full-time. They asked Elliot if he would consider joining their team as a VP. He was interested, but since his title at the prior company was already VP, and since Elliot had gained so much experience between his freelancing and his prior crypto job, we knew he deserved more. Elliot was able to take in this advice, because he knew we had *skin in the game.*

Through a very carefully constructed and strategic dance, we were able to convince the company that Elliot was CTO material. However, it didn't happen overnight.

Before we could prove to the company that Elliot was ready to be CTO, we had to point out to him that his people skills were going to need to be amped up—that's the kind of *Inner Vision* that talent management can provide. We showed Elliot that we were going to need to convince the company that he was ready to lead a large team.

Here's where our prior Super Vision really paid off: If not for the prior title bump we had pushed for, it's unlikely we would have been able to make this request. Ultimately, the company agreed to all Elliot's demands and requests. Much to our surprise (and the company's), Elliot opted not to take the job. He had other things he wanted to accomplish, in a totally different vertical.

We rolled with it. We knew that, in the new talent economy, people like Elliot have options. To work with them is to accept this basic fact, without reservations. And who's to say that following this 10xer down another path, one for which he was excited would not lead to an even better outcome?

We were on board to help Elliot pivot and carry out his vision. In order to do so, it was clear that he would need to learn a specific skill set he didn't have. Like a true 10xer, he was ready, willing, and able to seek further education—even as he was turning down a position to be CTO!

We introduced Elliot to one of our other 10x Management clients, a couple of guys who run a wonderful offshore dev shop. Simultaneously, he ended up on another project where he needed to manage a different offshore team. These teams gave Elliot rapid access to the skill sets he needed to master. Working with direct reports also afforded Elliot the opportunity to grow and improve his people skills, and to start practicing *360° management*, working with the end-customers, the team he was overseeing, and the guys who were providing him with a fresh education.

While delivering the coding for all the areas of the project he could handle, Elliot *switched hats* and was also managing the offshore teams to great effect. As of this writing, the project is still going strong and Elliot's relationship with his team and his colleagues is as solid as ever. And should the right company come calling, he is true CTO material, with blackbelt management skills to match his coding power.

Every step of the way, Elliot has had us on call, to help him identify his blind spots, to help him see thorny issues on the horizon before they arrive, and to advocate for him where needed. Elliot is now clearly in the Double-Hat World, knowing he has both the ability to run and manage large teams while also taking care of his own personal needs, including the desire for more education and more growth. Best of all, he's happy with the full picture, and flexible enough to be an individual contributor, a team member, or a team lead.

Elliot is just one of dozens of similar relationships we have with clients in both entertainment and tech. Working with people of his caliber over the years is what helped give us the vantage point with which the ideas of this book were born.

For each and every one of you, we hope you find and receive the kind of managerial guidance that can make a budding talent become 10x.

HIGH LEVEL BEST PRACTICES FOR COMPANIES WHEN APPROACHING A NEGOTIATION . . .

. . . With a W2 employee	. . . With a 1099 contractor
Learn as much as you can about what is important to a given candidate. Our Lifestyle Calculator is a great starting point. Without knowing what's important to a candidate, you can't possibly put forth an offer that will align with their career goals. Companies can create their own versions of the L.E.A.P. as a questionnaire to get from employees before making offers. This would be perceived as very progressive and employee-friendly.	Many companies use a one size fits all contract . . . one that's used for large consulting firms and for individual contractors. This makes no sense. Have two forms, one that is for a "company" that employs the contractor(s) that will work on your project, and one for small groups and individuals who are not on someone else's payroll. Ninety-day payment terms for an individual or small shop working on a project is completely out of line. Those payment terms may work for a larger consulting company, but would be untenable for an individual. Our best practice guide is that, for a company, 30-day payment terms are acceptable, and for small companies and individual contributors, 5-14 days should be standard form. And in the age of all things digital, if the idea of getting payments out in that time frame seems daunting, you might have some other issues to address.
Don't make a cookie cutter offer based on employees with "similar" skills. Use what you find out from the Lifestyle Calculator to inform where you add or subtract. Nothing is more off-putting than having a candidate feel like they are just a cog in a wheel. Learn enough about each candidate to make them feel unique.	When an engagement is a work for hire, as most contract engagements are, IP transfer should not occur until payment in full is made for the work conducted under said agreement. We encounter this all the time. Companies want IP transfer to occur regardless of payment for the creation of the IP. This makes no sense and provides zero protection to the contractor creating the IP. If this concept is a challenge for a company to address, the work-around is to pay in advance. This can be staged payments.

. . . With a W2 employee (cont.)	. . . With a 1099 contractor (cont.)
Don't make a cookie cutter offer . . . (cont.)	For example, you can pay weekly in advance of the upcoming week of work. At the end of said week, all IP created in that week is owned because the payment for that work has already occurred.
Evaluate how important a given candidate and skill set is to the strategic goals of the company and be willing to negotiate more or less aggressively based on that evaluation. Sometimes that may require you to adjust your internal payment structures or adjust how equity is earned (more on this below). For the right talent, these adjustments are well worth it.	Use contract forms that are as short and easy to execute as possible. We have dealt with single engagement contracts in excess of 50 pages—that's not acceptable. Our 10x Management form contract is six pages long. We've used this form in thousands of different engagements, from Fortune 500 companies, to small law firms, without any issues. Anything beyond ten pages is overkill. And for you lawyers out there, we've had numerous firms engage our 10x clients (tech talent) to do work for them and they all signed our agreement without issue. When you use a fair, concise, and logic-based agreement, things can run very smoothly.
Clearly explain company culture, values, and goals, and if a candidate is very important to you, allow them a chance to experience a little of the culture for themselves. Do this in a way that shows them that you heard what's important to them. If they are clearly not interested in ping-pong tables and nap pods, don't emphasize those elements. Put the emphasis on the things they do care about.	Make sure any agreement includes clear, mutually agreed upon communication expectations. When gigs go sideways, it's invariably because there is a misalignment in communications. We also stress to our clients and the companies contracting with them that addressing these issues up front before everyone starts working together is crucial and worth the extra effort, despite the fact that everyone wants to get going right away. Measure twice, cut once.

. . . With a W2 employee (cont.)	. . . With a 1099 contractor (cont.)
If you're not a publicly traded company and equity is a big part of your offering, give a prospective employee flexibility in when they need to exercise equity. You're likely using the carrot of equity to negotiate a lower cash offer, so be generous in how you allow your candidate to attain that equity. Help them understand the pros and cons of your offer. It's a complicated issue, and most people don't grasp the nuances without guidance. Having been burned so many times, many employees just totally discount the value of equity if it's not liquid.	Make more frequent payments. We invoice on a weekly basis so that the company engaging with our client gets smaller bills to pay, quicker access to the information about what work was conducted as part of that invoice, and payments can get into the accounts payable system more rapidly. This helps ensure that payments start flowing quickly and our client is not working for too long before seeing money. More important, this ensures that the invoices don't get so large that a delay in payment would create a major issue. Research shows that smaller, more frequent invoices help ensure payments are made on time. Additionally, it helps ensure more frequent transferring of IP when payments occur—another win-win situation.
Explain what is good and employee-friendly about your company. Don't take for granted that all companies do what you do. Know your competitive advantages, including the advantages of your product or service to those of your direct competitors. Also know the advantages your employment offering (including aspects such as long option periods for your equity, paid-for unused vacation time or allowing that time to roll over, unlimited vacation policy, etc.).	Ensure that your internal team is responding to contractor questions rapidly. More often than not, when our clients require more time to finish a specific build for a company, the delay is caused by members of the internal team not responding to code pushes that require approvals. Often we have to get involved and nudge for responses in order to help ensure that an engagement doesn't drag on unnecessarily.

TAKEAWAYS FROM CHAPTER 10

- Everyone at the negotiating table needs to represent themselves differently than they historically have. The balance has tipped in favor of the talent, at least for the talent that matters the most.

- Every negotiation is its own animal. Companies need to make offers based on the needs of an individual talent and not the general cohort that they've been trying to hire.

- Companies need to understand the broad lifestyle and employment goals of every candidate in order to make an offer customized to them. In addition to winning the talent wars, they may also save some money along the way because they know what a candidate wants which is not always cash. This will improve hiring rates and retention.

- Talent needs to familiarize themselves with the twenty-four elements in the Lifestyle Calculator and know which are relevant and most important to them, so that they are able to convey those needs to a prospective employer.

- Talent also needs to become adept at creating an Employment L.E.A.P. (List of Expectations and Priorities) document, to help present their wants and needs during the correct phase of negotiation.

- Companies need to be flexible in hiring W2 or 1099s, depending on the skill sets required and the ease with which talent can be procured to solve a given set of problems.

- Spectator management means learning to read the room in real time. It's the most essential "invisible" tool in contract negotiations of all kinds.

- The negotiator who can genuinely empathize with the other side of the table, and crafts deals with long-term relationships in mind, will ultimately build on their own reputation and have extra leverage when it's time to deal with difficult contract points. It gives them the ability to speak the right language and sell the right points.

INTRO **OUTRO**

THE WIN-WIN OF
THIS DOUBLE-HAT WORLD

I never lose. I either win or learn.
—NELSON MANDELA

F ull disclosure: When we were twenty-five years old and starting our management business together, we were mostly in it for the thrill of victory . . . and the money, of course. Maybe helping others was the cherry on top, but it certainly wasn't our prime motivator. To throw a successful keg party or get a band a gig at a bigger, better club was its own reward, and we were walking tall. Sure, we were occasionally fueled by the gratitude of a happy client, but we hadn't yet really learned just how powerful helping others could be.

Over time, however, hard work has a funny way of forcing you to grow up, sometimes despite yourself, and as we lived through bigger successes and deeper failures, we began to see a pattern emerge that we couldn't deny: Life was more satisfying, work more fulfilling, when we were able to make our clients' deepest goals become realities. It was more than just the thanks they expressed, and it certainly was more than the money we made. It was the sense that we had a hand in bringing dreams to reality and goals to fruition, together, as a team.

Hard to admit, but at first, it was a genuine surprise to discover that helping others is, in fact, the *most* rewarding part of the job. To be completely honest, we'd started four companies by the time we realized that everything we were doing was in the service of others. On the one hand, we may not be as smart as we'd like to think; on the other hand, we didn't have enough management of our own yet to help uncover our blind spots.

Now we know better. Now we know the source of our motivation. And it's *useful*—it literally powers us to do the work.

As daunting as it sometimes may be, *intention* goes hand in hand with talent-management work. What we do is as much an artform born of educated guesses as it is a hard, fast science. Ultimately, talent management is about humans, no matter what industry they work in, and humans are complicated and messy. Managing them, it turns out, is a challenging but emotionally proactive way to approach the world of work that celebrates your own victories through the victories of others. It also celebrates the capacity of humans to grow, work hard, evolve, learn, and ultimately prevail despite overwhelming odds.

And make no mistake: Their failures are your failures too. If you're smart, you'll let these failures grow into battle scars—your best teachers. They'll be there next time to help guide the way.

In writing this book, we have gotten to speak with some fascinating individuals, all of them true game changers. A few are new acquaintances but many are longtime friends and/or colleagues. On the whole, their day-to-day realities are very different from our own. Still, we've been thunderstruck by the universalities that have surfaced across industries and verticals, hearing the same basic messages from bank CEOs, from biotech coders, from life coaches and snack tycoons.

Here are just a few of the things they all seem to agree on:

- Where there is mutual trust and mutual respect, there is a greater chance for success.
- Talent has its own way of doing things that has to be honored. To let talent thrive, provide resources and get out of the way.
- Negotiation is never one-size-fits-all. To deliver at the negotiation table, you have to tune in to the real wants and desires of the other side with empathy and compassion.
- No matter how successful, rich, or powerful you are—or aren't—you'll need the guidance of an outside POV to properly learn and grow and to make your most important decisions.
- In teamwork, honesty is a priceless commodity and the only road to long-term trust.
- Team building happens when shared vision meets skin in the game.
- Empowerment goes hand in hand with accountability. Remove one and you lose the other.
- A genuine desire for mutual success is the only sane basis for any business partnership.
- High EQ is not "just as important" as high IQ. It's way more important.
- Empathy is the world's most powerful business tool.

Once you open yourself to these truths, these messages resurface everywhere you go.

As the future threatens even greater sweeping changes in the workplace, with technology developing an ever more acute ability to replicate human processes, we believe that the accent on empathy, talent, and mutual guidance can be a guiding light for many and a lifesaver for some.

The working world isn't always thought of as a primary source of spiritual beauty, but there *is* a meaningful elegance to the simple symbiotic nature of people working well together, especially when they are close enough and empathic enough to be able to switch hats. This is true whether those people are talent and manager, boss and subordinate, mentor and mentee, two parallel colleagues, or coach and client.

It goes like this: help the other person and you help yourself.

Time has taught us that the strength of our business model and the force behind our success is that it *all* comes from the success of others. In striving to be dream makers, we fulfilled our own by making theirs come true.

That's why we believe that win-win is the only real win.

ACKNOWLEDGMENTS

Michael and Rishon would like to thank:

The 10x Management, 10x Ascend, and Brick Wall Management teams (both current and past) for always striving to be 10x and enduring our endless book talk during this process: Griffith Adams, Michelle Humphries, Ryland Kenyon, Isaiah Machiz, Ben Miller, Michael Warner, Serena Yannello, and Sam Zeisler. And we'd especially like to thank all our 10x and Brick Wall clients for being the heart and soul of our ideas and execution. It's through our work with all of you that the concepts for this book were formulated. Thank you to Daniel Weizmann (Danny to us) for so many things, but most important, for tirelessly helping us put words and order to the chaos of the ideas in this book. We'd like to thank Altay Guvench for introducing us to the concept of 10x, for being our first coder client, and for co-founding 10x Management with us.

Michael, Rishon, and Daniel would like to thank:

The 10x-level team that made this book possible, starting with Lucinda Halpern and everyone at Lucinda Literary for agenting the agents with skill and passion, for helping us develop these ideas with care and finesse, and for providing us with true Inner and Future Vision. Tim Burgard for bringing us into HarperCollins Leadership and editing this work with patience and professionalism. Jeff James for believing in us and welcoming us into the HarperCollins Leadership family. Sicily Axton for helping to execute a wonderful marketing plan and introducing this book to the world. Mark Fortier and the team at Fortier Public Relations for your dedication and hard work. Christina Clifford for being the first person to encourage us to write and publish this book. Her early belief truly made a difference, and she was instrumental in introducing us to our literary agent. Margo Schupf who was also an early advocate and who gave us the confidence and guidance to get started. David Halpern for being wise enough to introduce us to Lucinda, and Geoff Shandler for his wonderful advice and generosity of time and spirit.

We thank all our interviewees:

Aaron Sylvan, Bryan Bishop, Daniel Lubetzky, Elvis Duran, Greg Sadetsky, James Diener, Jason Rubenstein, Jesse Lee, Jon Landau, Jonathan Lowenhar, Julie Hershman, Ken Levitan, Michael Counts, Ralph Perrine, Sam Botherton, Sara Ellis Conant, Scott Goldsmith, Shelley Seifert, Tom Poleman, Jeffrey Solomon, Barbara Carr, Audrey Weiner, and Vanessa Carlton. This book became 10x thanks to your contributions.

Michael would like to thank:

Jenny Kravat Solomon for doing so much for everyone and especially me. Lucy Solomon for proofreading this and using it. Rainen Solomon for being too smart for me. Arlene Guerra for being the first to instill some of these foundational lessons. Audrey Weiner for being the smartest person in the room. Jeffrey Solomon for being the wisest person in the room. Dave Marsh for being the first writer to show me the way. Barbara Carr for leading us to this path and giving us countless opportunities.

Rishon would like to thank:

A special thank you to my wife, Dr. Isabel Blumberg, whose early belief in this book was a genuine motivator ☺ and to my amazing boys, Alec and Luke Blumberg, who are true inspirations to me and are budding 10xers themselves—work hard, believe in yourself, and you can achieve whatever you set your mind to. I would like to give extra special thanks to my mother, Aviva Blumberg, who read every chapter of this book in real time and provided insightful feedback, and unyielding encouragement. Thank you to Nina and Larry Epstein, my wonderful and loving in-laws, for always supporting me. Thank you to Amy and Will Gadsden and Brian and Lauren Epstein for being the best brothers- and sisters-in-law anyone could hope for. And thank you to my beautiful and talented nieces, Lindsay, Merrill, Lucy, Chelsea, and Edie, who make me laugh and keep me on my toes. I would like to thank Michael for being my partner in crime since third grade, and Daniel, whom I've known all my life. This book would never have happened if not for the tireless efforts of both of you.

Daniel would like to thank:

Clover Chadwick, Max Weizmann, Rama Weizmann, and Aviva Blumberg for their enduring love, patience, and support. He'd also like to thank Michael and Rishon for introducing him to a complex, captivating new world and a wealth of truly useful ideas.

ENDNOTES

CHAPTER 1
Understanding the 10xer

1. For a four-minute animated video summarizing the history of Silicon Valley: https://www.businessinsider.com/silicon-valley-history-technology-industry-animated-timeline-video-2017-5.
2. Emma Goldberg, "'Techlash' Hits College Campuses," *The New York Times*, January 11, 2020. Accessed at https://www.nytimes.com/2020/01/11/style/college-tech-recruiting.html?smid=nytcore-ios-share.
3. Jeanne G. Harris and Allan E. Alter, "California Dreaming," Outlook issue No. 1, Accenture, 2014. Accessed at https://www.accenture.com/_acnmedia/Accenture/Conversion-Assets/Outlook/Documents/1/Accenture-Outlook-California-Dreaming-Corporate-Culture-Silicon-Valley.pdf.
4. Harris and Alter, "California Dreaming."
5. Nish Acharya, "Why Corporate America Finally Embraced Silicon Valley," *Forbes*, May 31, 2019. Accessed at https://www.forbes.com/sites/nishacharya/2019/05/31/why-corporate-america-finally-embraced-silicon-valley/#37d9156515dc.
6. Joanie Faletto, "You Can Build 'Deep Work' Skills to Increase Productivity, Curiosity.com, February 21, 2018. Accessed at https://curiosity.com/topics/you-can-build-deep-work-skills-to-increase-productivity-curiosity?utm_campaign=daily-digest&utm_source=sendgrid&utm_medium=email.
7. Kathryn Vasel, "These Employers Don't Care When or Where You Work," CNN Business, October 18, 2019. Accessed at https://www.cnn.com/2019/10/18/success/results-only-work-place/index.html?utm_term=link&utm_content=2019-12-26T04%3A00%3A15&utm_source=fbCNN&utm_medium=social.
8. Daniel Terdiman, "How A Hacker Helped the Coast Guard Rescue Victims of Hurricane Harvey," *Fast Company*, September 30, 2017. Accessed at https://www.fastcompany.com/40475242/how-a-hacker-helped-the-coast-guard-rescue-victims-of-hurricane-harvey.
9. Adi Gaskell, "The Key to Solving Future Skills Challenges," *Forbes*, January 2, 2019. Accessed at https://www.forbes.com/sites/adigaskell/2019/01/02/solving-future-skills-challenges/#6093ef5e47d9.

10. Alex Hearn, "The Two-Pizza Rule and the Secret of Amazon's Success," *The Guardian*, April 24, 2018. Accessed at https://www.theguardian.com/technology/2018/apr/24/the-two-pizza-rule-and-the-secret-of-amazons-success.

11. "Steve Jobs in His Own Words," CNET, October 5, 2011. Accessed at https://www.cnet.com/news/steve-jobs-in-his-own-words/.

12. "OKR: Objectives and Key Results," Weekdone.com. Accessed at https://weekdone.com/resources/objectives-key-results.

13. Anna Liotta, "Generational Keynote Speaker Demo," Video, 1:07–1:25. Accessed at https://youtu.be/icQWsSWM24Y.

CHAPTER 2

The Bespoke Boss

1. Eryn Paul, "7 Signs Your Boss Is Old School—And How to Deal with It," Knote (undated). Accessed at http://science.knote.com/2015/02/06/7-signs-boss-old-school-deal/.

2. John Sullivan, "Why Your Firm Has a Talent Shortage Explained (Bluntly)," ERE, August 5, 2019. Accessed at https://www.ere.net/why-your-firm-has-a-talent-shortage-explained-bluntly/.

3. Anne Fisher, "An Algorithm May Decide Your Next Pay Raise," *Fortune*, July 14, 2019. Accessed at https://fortune-com.cdn.ampproject.org/c/s/fortune.com/2019/07/14/artificial-intelligence-workplace-ibm-annual-review/amp/.

4. Jesy Odio, "The Magician: The dFm's Jesse Lee," *LA Canvas*, April 14, 2016. Accessed at https://lacanvas.com/the-magician-the-dfms-jesse-lee/.

5. Sheila Marikar, "LA's New Hype King Has Cracked How Millennials Spend," Bloomberg, November 12, 2017. Accessed at https://www.bloomberg.com/news/features/2017-11-14/la-s-new-hype-king-has-cracked-how-millennials-spend.

CHAPTER 3

Success and Sabotage—The Manageability Continuum

1. Jörgen Sundberg, "What Is the True Cost of Hiring a Bad Employee?" The Undercover Recruiter. Accessed at February 25, 2012, https://theundercoverrecruiter.com/infographic-what-cost-hiring-wrong-employee/.

2. Will Wei, "Tony Hsieh: Bad Hires Have Cost Zappos Over $100 Million," *Business Insider*, October 25, 2010. Accessed at https://www.businessinsider.com/tony-hsieh-making-the-right-hires-2010-10.

3. Jackie Cooperman, "New Studies Suggest Emotional Intelligence Boosts Productivity," Worth, August 13, 2019. Accessed at https://www.worth.com/new-studies-suggest-emotional-intelligence-boosts-productivity/.

CHAPTER 4

Super Visionaries

1. Steven Stosny, "Blind Spots: Know What Your Partner Is Reacting to When You Argue," *Psychology Today*, May 13, 2018. Accessed at https://www.psychologytoday .com/us/blog/anger-in-the-age-entitlement/201805/blind-spots.
2. "Johari Window Model and Free Diagrams," BusinessBalls. Accessed at https://www .businessballs.com/self-awareness/johari-window-model-and-free-diagrams/.
3. Jessica Stillman, "Get to Know Yourself Better with the Johari Window," Curiosity .com, September 4, 2019. Accessed at https://curiosity.com/topics/get-to-know -yourself-better-with-the-johari-window-curiosity/.
4. Alexandra Sleator, "5 Ways to Find Your Blind Spots," Ivy Exec. Accessed at https:// www.ivyexec.com/career-advice/2014/5-ways-find-blind-spots/.

CHAPTER 5

To Be Gained, It Must Be Earned

1. Paul Thagard, "What Is Trust?" *Psychology Today*, October 9, 2018. Accessed at https://www.psychologytoday.com/us/blog/hot-thought/201810/what-is-trust.
2. Thomas Oppong, "An FBI Behaviour Expert Explains How to Quickly Build Trust With Anyone," Medium, August 16, 2019. Accessed at https://medium.com /personal-growth/an-fbi-behaviour-expert-explains-how-to-quickly-build-trust -with-anyone-94a05be01cea.
3. K. Huang, M. Yeomans, A. W. Brooks, J. Minson, and F. Gino, "It Doesn't Hurt to Ask: Question-asking Increases Liking," *Journal of Personality and Social Psychology*, September 2017. Accessed at https://www.hbs.edu/faculty/Pages/item.aspx?num =52115.

CHAPTER 6

Skin in the Game

1. Hollie McKay, "Entertainment Pros: Most Hollywood Moms Should Be Moms, Not Momagers," Fox News, May 10, 2013. Accessed at https://www.foxnews.com /entertainment/entertainment-pros-most-hollywood-moms-should-be-moms-not -momagers.
2. 10x Talent Nation Book Graph Skin in The Game/Objectivity. Accessed at https:// docs.google.com/spreadsheets/d/1GjtQZDD8swT_3ncKmiovxB0VX_AN7oW kLl9avTBngyQ/edit#gid=519861808.

CHAPTER 7

The Third Party Effect

1. Antonio Regalado, "The World's First Gattaca Baby Tests Are Finally Here," *MIT Technology Review*, November 8, 2019. Accessed at https://www.technologyreview .com/s/614690/polygenic-score-ivf-embryo-dna-tests-genomic-prediction-gattaca /?utm_source=newsletters&utm_medium=email&utm_campaign=the_download .unpaid.engagement.
2. Richard Feloni, "Late Oracle CEO Mark Hurd Explained to Us One of the Unspoken Attributes of a Great Leader," *Business Insider*, October 20, 2019. Accessed at https://www.businessinsider.com/oracle-ceo-mark-hurd-on-leadership-2019-4.
3. Firas Kittaneh, "3 Ways Leaders Can Become Outstanding Advocates for Their Team," *Inc.*, September 25, 2018. Accessed at https://www.inc.com/firas-kittaneh /3-ways-leaders-can-become-outstanding-advocates-for-their-team.html.

CHAPTER 8

360° Management

1. Laura Delizonna, "High-Performing Teams Need Psychological Safety. Here's How to Create It," *Harvard Business Review*, August 24, 2017. Accessed at https://hbr .org/2017/08/high-performing-teams-need-psychological-safety-heres-how-to -create-it.
2. Deborah Holstein, "Some People Hate Being Managed—What Organizations (And Managers) Need to Do Instead," Betterworks.com, March 29, 2018. Accessed at https://blog.betterworks.com/people-hate-being-managed-what-organizations -and-managers-need-to-do-instead/.
3. Richard Feloni, "Inside Zappos CEO Tony Hsieh's Radical Management Experiment That Prompted 14% of Employees to Quit," *Business Insider*, May 16, 2015. Accessed at https://www.businessinsider.com/tony-hsieh-zappos-holacracy-management -experiment-2015-5.

CHAPTER 9

The Ultimate Skill—Donning the Double Hat

1. Jack Zenger and Joseph Folkman, "The Ideal Praise-to-Criticism Ratio," *Harvard Business Review*, March 15, 2013. Accessed at https://hbr.org/2013/03/the-ideal -praise-to-criticism.
2. Sarah Kessler, "You Probably Should Have Majored in Computer Science," Quartz, March 10, 2017. Accessed at https://qz.com/929275/you-probably-should-have -majored-in-computer-science/.
3. Allison Berry, "50 Highest Paying College Majors," GlassDoor.com, July 18, 2018. Accessed at https://www.glassdoor.com/blog/50-highest-paying-college-majors/.

4. Kumar (pseudonymous blogger), "USCIS News: H1B Visa 2020 Cap Reached for Regular Quota," May 25, 2019. Accessed at https://redbus2us.com/uscis-news-h1b -visa-2020-cap-reached-for-regular-quota/.
5. Hope Bear, "How One Local Tech Company Is Tackling the STEM Shortage," Access blog, Technical.ly, December 2, 2019. Accessed at https://technical.ly/philly /2019/12/02/aweber-tackling-stem-talent-shortage-mentorship-education -women-youth/.

CHAPTER 10

The Evolution of the Deal

1. Lisa D. McNary, "The Term 'Win-Win' in Conflict Management: A Classic Case of Misuse and Overuse," *The Journal of Business Communication* 40:2, April 2003. Accessed at https://www.questia.com/library/journal/1G1-100390016/the-term -win-win-in-conflict-management-a-classic.

INDEX

ABOUT THE AUTHORS

For two decades, Michael Solomon and Rishon Blumberg have been revolutionizing the field of talent management, first guiding the careers of rock stars, then bringing their unique managerial acumen to tech talent and entrepreneurs.

Native New Yorkers and close childhood friends who got their entrepreneurial start in the '80s throwing parties and selling T-shirts, Michael and Rishon founded Brick Wall Management in 1995, representing musicians like John Mayer, Citizen Cope, Vanessa Carlton, and others. Brick Wall artists have been nominated for and won multiple Grammy Awards with collectively more than twelve million albums sold. Brick Wall has also grown into a successful consulting business that advises clients in many aspects of the arts—from Emmy Award-winning songwriters to producers, directors, and entertainment-related companies.

As the decline of the record industry in the first decade of the twenty-first century became apparent, Rishon and Michael set their sights on expanding into the tech world. With the creation of 10x Management in 2012, they changed the way top-level programmers could find work in the fast-moving tech landscape. By bringing the business model of sports and entertainment representation to the tech world, 10x has become an invaluable resource for companies seeking coveted tech experts: Yelp, BirchBox, Verizon, HSBC, Google, Facebook, MIT, BMW, and Vice, to name a few. In 2019 with the addition of 10x Ascend, they expanded their offerings to include helping senior tech talent negotiate full time, W2

Rodeph Sholom 1978 featuring Rishon Blumberg (left) and Michael Solomon (right)

Rishon Blumberg (left) and Michael Solomon (right) circa 1987

compensation packages. Their companies have been featured in dozens of news outlets where both founders regularly share opinions (*The New York Times, The New Yorker, Harvard Business Review, Wall Street Journal, Forbes, CNN, Bloomberg, BusinessWeek, Fast Company, MSNBC, ABC, Nightline, The Today Show, Wired, TechCrunch, Mashable, HuffPost, The Guardian, The Economist,* and *Inc.,* to name a few) including a seven-page feature in *The New Yorker.*

Michael and Brick Wall also serve as the pro-bono administrator for The Kristen Ann Carr Fund (KACF), a nonprofit dedicated to finding treatments and a cure for sarcoma as well as improving the lives of all cancer patients. It was founded in 1993 after Michael's girlfriend of four years, Kristen Carr, lost her battle with sarcoma. He was honored at The Kristen Ann Carr Fund's Twentieth Anniversary Night to Remember in 2013. The KACF inspired Michael to co-found Musicians On Call (MOC), a national nonprofit that brings live music to hospital patients at their bedsides. Playing for more than 700,000 patients to date, MOC currently runs in twenty-six cities nationally and is growing at an unprecedented rate. Michael received the 2014 President's Volunteer Service Award from President Obama and was named NY1 New Yorker of the Week for his work with MOC. In 2019, Michael was honored at Musicians On Call's twentieth anniversary celebration with the Lifetime Achievement Award where MOC also renamed its volunteer musician award after him. He was also in the bestselling philanthropy book *The Art of Giving.* Michael's diverse management and marketing expertise makes him a sought-after voice. He has spoken at SXSW and CMJ, and has been a guest lecturer on music and philanthropy at New York University. He's also been a mentor and speaker at the Founder Institute, and appeared at numerous events and conferences.

A born and bred Manhattanite, Michael moved to Montclair, New Jersey, in 2014 with his awesome wife, Jenny, and two fantastic kids, Lucy and Rainen.

•   •   •

A graduate of the Wharton School with a degree in entrepreneurial management, Rishon is a trusted voice in discussions about the future of work and the Talent Economy. He began his career in concert promotion—first at Nederlander Concerts and then Delsener/Slater Enterprises, which later became Live Nation.

Rishon has a keen business sense that drives him to find the best talent and make a lasting impact. Additionally, he thrives on doing good and improving people's lives. He also acts as administrator for The Kristen Ann Carr Fund for sarcoma research and sits on the advisory board of Musicians On Call. Rishon has presented about the Talent Economy at TEDx, has appeared numerous times on television (Bloomberg Television, BBC) and has been published in the *Harvard Business Review*. In 2017, he was featured on the cover of the Wharton Alumni Club of New York's Quarterly Magazine. In addition, Rishon has presented at SXSW, NYU, and for the Wharton Alumni Association.

He has spent many years coaching his sons'(Alec and Luke) sports teams to victory (or otherwise)—arguably his greatest achievement to date.

Game Changer is Michael and Rishon's first book.

Daniel Weizmann's writing has appeared in the *Los Angeles Times*, *Billboard*, Buzz, Jewish Journal AP Newswire, and several anthologies including *Turn Up the Radio* and *Drinking with Bukowski*. He has an International MBA from Bar Ilan University.